"The way to approach this book is the way in which Moses approached the burning bush: with reverence and openness. Expect to hear your name called out from this *Handful of Fire.*"

Macrina Wiederkehr, OSB.
Author, *Gold in Your Memories*

"Carole Marie Kelly, with the simple wisdom of St. Francis of Assisi and other mystics, has had the kindness and courage to invite us to the 'one thing necessary.' Carole Marie shows the gift of a good teacher offering us stories from her own life so that we might listen to the rich depths of our own. Her readers will quickly become seekers returning to the one well of life and Scriptures, which always has fresh waters for those who take the time to stop and drink. Our author humbly and humorously points us to this renewing source."

Daniel Riley, OFM
Mt. Irenaeus
Franciscan Mountain Retreat

"This is a fine resource for those who know they are ready to read the Bible for themselves, but still don't dare to go there alone! Reading Sr. Carole Marie's meditations gave me the sense that I was sharing the intimate space of her retreat cabin with her. Hers is a gentle, persuasive guidance into the sometimes fearful, often misty encounter with Scripture. A few evenings with this book will give you the benefits of a retreat, without the expense."

Alice Camille
Author, *God's Word Is Alive*

A
Handful
of FIRE

Praying Contemplatively
with Scripture

CAROLE MARIE KELLY

TWENTY-THIRD PUBLICATIONS
A Division of Bayard   MYSTIC, CT 06355

Twenty-Third Publications
A Division of Bayard
185 Willow Street
P.O. Box 180
Mystic, CT 06355
(860) 536-2611
(800) 321-0411

ISBN:1-58595-126-9
Library of Congress Catalog Card Number: 00-135467
Printed in the U.S.A.

Contents

Part One • Approaching the Fire

Part Two • Touching the Fire

Part Three · Being Fire

Foreword

This book is an invitation to a life of intimacy with the Word of God. To read the Scriptures prayerfully, in the way that is suggested here, is to discover the Word as actuality, as presence. It is to embark upon a journey of progressive union with God.

The Word of God introduces us into a new world of inner experience; it is the door to the discovery of a new self. These extraordinary statements are sanctioned by a tradition of thousands of years, by an experience which is renewed in each age. It is renewed once again today, when the practice of lectio divina, or the prayerful and meditative reading of the Scriptures, once again becomes common. The wisdom dimensions of Christianity once again begin to emerge in our western world as we emerge from the confinement of our modern rationalism, breaking through the walls that have come to enclose our everyday consciousness.

If the Word opens to us an inner world, a depth dimension of self and life, it also becomes the center of a new world around us. The divine Word is not only word but Spirit, the divine energy which is manifest both within our hearts and in the history that flows around us. Jesus, Mark tells us, taught with authority (power, *exousia* in the original Greek), and not as the scribes and Pharisees. Jesus, John tells us, is himself the Word of God. The divine Word is ever filled with the divine Spirit, and Jesus' words carry the fullness and power of that Spirit. This is true today as it was in the time when Jesus walked upon the earth, and in the time when the apostles preached the word and the gospels themselves were written.

Today, once again, we become aware of these dimensions of depth and power that are inseparable from the biblical revelation. The depth, the light, and the energy are centered in the Word of God which has become a human person in Jesus Christ, and has then been given to us in the gospels and the other writings of the New Testament. We are invited once again to become initiated into a wisdom Christianity, grounded in the biblical word, which grows from a meditative reading of both Testaments and is vitally centered in "the mystery," the event of Christ.

The key to this dwelling with the Scriptures—a reading which becomes life—is participation. This is a way of knowing quite different from the objective knowing which has prevailed since the dawn of the scientific age in the West. It is a knowing with experience, but more: this experience corresponds to an actual union with that which is known. The experience is an awareness of the coming forth of a new self, a new person who is at once oneself and God, oneself and Christ. This is the knowledge of faith which flashes forth in the gospel stories when someone encounters Jesus. In one moment Peter, or Nathanael, or Magdalene discover God's Anointed One in Jesus, and—more obscurely—their own self-awakening to an inner divinity which is at once new and eternal. This book is an introduction to a participative reading of the Scriptures. Although this is an activity that demands of us practice and some patience, it is a reading and knowing which is ultimately most simple and most natural.

In the tradition of Christian wisdom which continued until the beginning of modern times, union with the Word was imagined as proceeding in four stages, called in the original Latin *lectio, meditatio, oratio,* and *contemplatio,* or reading, reflection, prayer, and silent contemplation. Lectio, the slow and meditative reading of the Scriptures, requires a gearing down from our ordinary rapid processing of information in a text. Meditatio is the silent rumination, the turning over of the Word in the mind and heart, which opens its inner fullness. Oratio is the Word become prayer, pouring forth from the heart. Contemplatio is a resting within the Word beyond the movement of thought, the delightful stillness of union. You will find the chapters of this book moving freely among these four levels of personal union with the Word.

How does one enter into the way of Christian wisdom? How does one begin to read the diverse and massive biblical writings in depth? It is well to seek first the center of the Scriptures, to study the mystery of Christ as it appears in the gospels and the Pauline letters. Setting out from this center and returning to it from time to time, one can explore the world of the two testaments.

The great principle is this: simply to fall in love with the scriptural Word; to embrace it with the whole of oneself; to become intimate with the Word, live with it, relate to it as food, drink, companion. If you do this, you will not be disappointed. More important than clear ideas, than answers, are presence and relationship. Through your relationship with the book comes understanding. Linger with the text— with a scene, a parable—silently and patiently, as with a friend. The communication is gradual, often imperceptible, but deep and broad. Do not let yourself become too frustrated when you don't seem to "get it." The participation, the nourishing, the progressive union, is going on anyway.

Seek out the "hot spots," the places in the Scripture where the words are full of energy for you. Be sensitive to the allure of the text and of elements in the text—the figure of Jesus and his words, these particular words that light up for you at this moment. Feel for the warmth that reveals an area of attraction and of energy for you. This energy contains light and understanding, but you don't have to extract it right away. Stay with it. More than knowledge, become aware of the radiance, the field of energy and light around a scene, a text, a saying.

. This book is the fruit of the personal experience and reflection of someone who has lived for many years in contemplative solitude, spending much time in the reading of the Scriptures and in prayer. Sr. Carole Marie's book is an invitation to pursue the same journey into the heart of the Scriptures—and into the depth of your own heart, where the divine light and fire dwell. You will not find here the historical and textual information, or the critical analysis, that you would expect in a standard professional biblical commentary (as, for instance, the *New Jerome Biblical Commentary*). Rather, this volume traces the process of personal union with the divine Word present in the Scriptures.

As you read the chapters which follow, your own Bible should never be out of reach. If Sr. Carole Marie's work is effective, you will gradually find yourself experiencing an immediate relationship with the scriptural Word, a relationship in which you are gently illumined, enkindled, and moved as you go on. The words and scenes of the gospels will become your own, as did the words and actions of Jesus' life for Mary as she "pondered them in her heart."

Words and concepts that you will encounter again and again in these chapters are: hidden, stillness, silence, resting, waiting, listening, presence, mystery, depth, interiority, union, darkness, faith, inner knowing, transformation, wonder and desire, light, fire, and life. These ideas and images represent the shapes and colors, the rhythms and tones, the motions and encounters, that characterize this inner country of the Word. Beneath the lively surface of the biblical land of vari-colored human stories and historic conflicts, dwells the eternal light and fire that lives within your own awakenings and struggles, in the depths of your own heart.

As you read Sr. Carole Marie's book, may you begin to discover the Scriptures as your own. As you continue to dwell with the two Testaments, may you progressively find yourself to be one with the Word.

Bruno Barnhart, CamOSB
New Camaldoli Hermitage
January 28, 2000

Acknowledgments

My thanks are offered to all those who have unknowingly inspired my own love for Scripture by sharing their reflections on the infinite facets of the word of God.

I am especially grateful to Bruno Barnhart, CamOSB, without whose wisdom, penetrating insight, and patience this book could not have been written. His continual willingness to review each chapter and offer suggestions as well as theological perspective truly made this project a deepening spiritual experience for me.

The Sisters of my Franciscan religious community have given me guidance and support for many years, but I want to express my appreciation in particular for their enabling my response to a call to contemplative life in solitude for the past twenty years. The thoughts I have shared in this book have their roots in that solitude.

I also want to acknowledge and thank all who have participated in my retreats or asked me for spiritual guidance. It was the difficulty some expressed in reflecting on Scripture and their longing to enter into a contemplative listening to the sacred words that led to my writing this book. I pray that it may lead them to share my enthusiasm for scriptural prayer.

Introduction

It can be startling to realize that Sacred Scripture, which we hold in
our hands so lightly, encloses a luminous fire, a divine energy poised
ready to draw us into its radiant mystery. Its flames burn so quietly
that we experience their warmth only if we move beneath the surface
of the words and rest there for a time. The Word of God awaits our
attentive presence, urging us to draw near, yet we sometimes hesitate
to read Scripture because we do not always find the warmth and richness of meaning that we desire. In fact, at times we seem to encounter
only silence and emptiness, so we close the book.

This is an experience well known to many. Yet paradoxically, an
inner knowing and strength can arise out of that very silence, a fullness out of the emptiness. This can be difficult to recognize at first.
We must become accustomed to the quiet, feel at home in the darkness, relax into the emptiness, so that we can be attuned to the subtle
movements of the Spirit within us. Then we may be aware of interior
feelings of peace, yearning, an expansion of spirit, or an intuitive
sense of presence. We may, however, not feel anything! That, too, is
grace, for it calls forth a pure faith which, in itself, is a touch of the
Spirit. Each experience is a unique communication between the Spirit
and the soul that is difficult to describe. Just as there are no words
adequate to express the feeling of intimacy between man and woman,
human words cannot begin to describe the interior knowing that
illumines the union of the soul with God.

Of course, there are many occasions while reading Scripture when
we do receive a clear gift of insight, a deeper understanding of the passage we are reading. Then it is natural to come away feeling nourished. The challenge is to learn also to recognize the more subtle ways

in which we are touched with divine grace.

Frequently I have heard people say, "I don't get anything out of Scripture," or "Scripture is beyond me because I've never studied it. I wouldn't even know where to begin reading it." Still others complain of the violence in the texts, or the sexist language. All of these thoughts can become barriers to the reading of Scripture.

In this book, I do not propose to respond specifically to each of these concerns, but to suggest ways of moving beyond them in order to find light and life in the Word of God. If we begin by reading the scriptural passages with which we are most familiar and comfortable, and reflecting on them in ways suggested in these chapters, ways that lead to deeper prayer, these barriers will gradually fade. As we begin to realize that we are "getting something out of Scripture," even though it may not be what we expected, we will find that our love for the Word surpasses understanding, and that what we encounter consumes our resistance to reading Scripture.

The chapters of Part One introduce various methods of approaching a scriptural text to uncover its hidden meaning. Lady Wisdom is introduced as a treasured companion so she may be recognized in the many ways in which we encounter her. Then suggestions are offered to help the reader see beyond the familiar in a scriptural passage, discern and accept personal insight, and respect the changing rhythms of prayer. These chapters are meant to entice the person who is not accustomed to reading Scripture to begin the practice, and to rekindle the enthusiasm of those who already read Scripture so they may find fresh fascination with the text.

In Part Two, the reader journeys briefly through diverse genres of sacred Scripture: psalms, prophecies, parables, stories, and historical narratives. An example of each genre serves as the theme of a chapter so that the reader has the experience of reading that type of text, reflecting on its meaning, and moving toward contemplation. Then several biblical narratives are recalled in which women and men encounter God in various ways that often mirror our own experience. These chapters offer an immersion in the actual process of scriptural prayer that is meant to encourage the reader to continue with the practice.

The chapters of Part Three point to the heart of the scriptural message. Contemplation of the mystery found in the luminous words of Scripture can enable us to know the unitive reality of God more intimately, and in that knowing, to realize that we are in fact united to God. In the words of Julian of Norwich, "Our soul is oned to God....between God and the soul, there is no between." Oneness with God is also a oneness with all of humanity! The myriad implications of this truth serve to raise our awareness of the injustice, violence, and poverty that surround us and to move us to a response.

The experience of reading each chapter of the book will be enhanced when the reader spends prayerful moments reflecting on the scriptural texts considered and listening to their reverberations in his or her heart, for that is where the whisper of wisdom may be heard.

The thoughts you will find on these pages reflect my personal enthusiasm and love for Scripture. I pray that as you read them you may find your own longing for intimacy with the living Word of God renewed and deepened.

I have avoided gender specific language as much as possible, but there are occasions when the limitations of English grammar make inclusive language awkward. I rely on the understanding of the reader at such times.

PART ONE

Approaching
the FIRE

"Come and see."

Invited by the Spirit
to open Sacred Scripture,
we begin to read a familiar text,
longing to know the warmth
of its inner fire.

Exploring the paths that lead
to the mystery
beneath the words,
we find our way,
and draw near to the infinite wisdom.

We pause there.
In the stillness of our heart
we experience the subtle movement of grace
that attunes us
to the whispering
of the Spirit.

1

Hidden Treasure

Beyond the Familiar

One winter, when the snow was very deep, a poor boy
had to gather firewood to warm the cabin. He trudged
into the forest, dragging his sled behind him. When he
had piled enough wood on his sled, he was very cold,
so he decided to make a fire to warm himself. As the boy
began scraping away the snow, he found a small golden
key. Where there is a key, he thought, there must be a
lock, so he dug into the ground and found a little iron
chest with a tiny keyhole. Trembling with excitement, he
put the key into the rusty keyhole and slowly turned the
golden key.

"The Golden Key," The Brothers Grimm

And then....That cannot be the end of the story. Stories do not end
that way. Nevertheless, it does, and the Brothers Grimm tell us that
now we must wait until the boy unlocks the chest and opens it.
"That's when we'll learn what wonderful things he found."

Yet the story has not really ended. I remember it. So many stories
like this one leave us with a lingering sense of mystery. That day, the
next week, the next year, I could still imagine what was in the old iron
chest, and wonder how it changed the boy's life. I once told the story
to a group of adults and asked them what they thought the boy found
in the chest. One said it must have been filled with ancient gold
coins, while another insisted there were jewels, rubies, sapphires, and

diamonds. A pessimist was sure the contents were worthless. He saw moldy, decaying documents that had lost their value. The adults had heard stories like this before and were quite sure of the ending, so this tale held no mystery for them, no magic. They were obviously bored and wondered why I had told them such a story.

Children, however, played my finish-the-story game very different-ly, using their imaginations to fill the treasure chest with visions of candy bars, toy dragons, and tiny green frogs that leapt out when they opened the lid. They felt the anticipation of the boy and participated in his excitement. Each time they heard about the old treasure chest, they could find something new inside! The children were able to do more than finish the story, because the story came to life inside of them. They filled in the untold parts, listening between the words, feeling the boy's cold hands and enthusiasm, and discovering their own hidden treasure.

While the adults had stayed on the outside, passively listening to the words, the children identified with the boy and crawled inside the story. They lived it while the adults only listened to it. The words of the story took root in the children's imagination, while the adults measured it against other stories, and gave unthinking, learned responses to the too familiar theme of a buried treasure chest.

Scripture is filled with such unfinished stories tarnished by repeti-tion. So often we are told only a fragment of someone's life or offered a glimpse into a transforming experience. How did the Israelites spend their years in exile? What did Mary do after the Ascension? Did the man born blind follow Jesus after he was healed? And what about the rich young man? Did he find the courage to sell his possessions? We might even wonder how Noah and his family began a new life after the flood. What ever happened to Mary Magdalene?

Scriptural stories go on and on unless someone pretends to know exactly what happened and closes the doors of our intuitive sense that can lead us ever deeper into the mystery where we begin to hear the whisper of the Spirit. In fact, John ends his gospel by reminding us that it is not complete because he has recorded only a few of the significant episodes of Jesus' ministry:

But there are also many other things that Jesus did;
if every one of them were written down,
I suppose that the world itself could not contain
the books that would be written. (Jn 21:25)

John's gospel displays his artistry of giving us just enough information to enflame our hearts and include us in the scene. That is why the words he wrote are still brimming with life. There is so much for us to hear as we listen to the gospel message because it is vibrant with mystery and infinite in wisdom. We are drawn into the action because Christ's life continues within us.

The gospel of John opens with "In the beginning," a timeless expression that reminds me of "Once upon a time" and entices me to continue reading. Then he tells us of the dwelling place of the Word of God before the Word became flesh and lived among us. The whole prologue (Jn 1:1–18) is filled with astonishing statements about Jesus that have lost their luster for many of us because we read them in one gulp without pausing to consider the ramifications and intensity of each phrase; for example:

All things came into being through him…
yet the world did not know him.
We have seen his glory….
From his fullness we have all received,
grace upon grace.

He concludes this introduction with an enticement to continue reading the gospel, telling us that "No one has ever seen God. It is God the only Son, who is close to the Father's heart, who has made him known" (Jn 1:18).

That statement alone can allure us, enkindling a desire to enter into the stories of the life of Jesus, that we might learn to know him and to know his Father. Yet we can be as slow to learn as the apostles were! The evening before Jesus died, "Philip said to him, 'Lord, show us the Father, and we will be satisfied.' Jesus said to him, 'Have I been with you all this time, Philip, and you still do not know me? Whoever has seen me has seen the Father'" (Jn 14:8–9). Philip had certain expectations of what Yahweh must be like, expectations garnered from a lifetime of listening to others explain the Scriptures to him.

What do we expect? Is our image of the Father carried over from our childhood when we perceived him as an all-seeing, judging, punitive God? Or do we think of the Father as a loving, forgiving God, one who rejoices in the return of his prodigal child? How did we form these impressions? Have they frozen in place? This may be true of our impression of many aspects of Scripture: they remain set in the interpretation we once heard, and frozen in familiarity. We can soften them and shape them anew by approaching the fire of the Holy Spirit that permeates the inspired words.

For example, one day John the Baptist saw Jesus walking by and pointed him out to his disciples, exclaiming, "Look, here is the Lamb of God!" (Jn 1:36). Two disciples decided to follow Jesus, probably out of curiosity, and were surprised when Jesus turned and asked them, "What are you looking for?" Not knowing exactly what to say, they replied, "Rabbi (which translated means "teacher"), where are you staying?"

Andrew and the other disciple, possibly John the evangelist himself, had no idea of the depth of the question they had asked. It seemed so simple. When Jesus looked at them and answered, "Come and see" (Jn 1:37–39), their lives were turned upside down and inside out! That was only the beginning of the story. They spent the rest of the day with Jesus, and we are left to imagine what they talked about. What was the hidden treasure that Jesus revealed as he slowly opened his heart to them? Perhaps he told them of his eternal dwelling in his Father, of his desire to make his home among us, or perhaps it was his very presence which spoke silent volumes to the two visitors.

We've read that story before. Can we read it again with the wonder of a child, or does our adult memory fill in the spaces with what we have heard before, so we close the book, perhaps afraid of listening to what Jesus might say to us now? Once when some Pharisees had been challenging Jesus, and his disciples asked even more questions about the discussion, Jesus called attention to the little children saying, "Truly I tell you, whoever does not receive the kingdom of God as a little child will never enter it"(Mk 10:15). That may be a clue to our reading of the Word of God: whoever does not read it as a little child will never enter it. The beauty of Scripture is that it is always new as we read it in the eternal now.

And then there are the multiple facets of the texts that we can only glimpse if we pause to allow the beauty that lies hidden in the spaces between the words to emerge. That unseen, unspoken wisdom awaits our prayerful receptivity and resonates in our hearts as it touches us personally. A phrase from a psalm may unexpectedly affect us, for it expresses our own deepest desire: "O God, you are my God, I seek you, my soul thirsts for you" (Ps 63:1). Jesus' words to the Samaritan woman, "If you only knew..." can spring forth from the page as if spoken directly to us, leaving an inexpressible longing in our hearts (Jn 4:7–10). The profound wisdom that reverberates within the sacred text is never fully expressed because there are no human words with which to describe it, but it is there waiting for us to discover.

> For there is nothing hidden, except to be disclosed;
> nor is anything secret, except to come to light.
> Let anyone with ears to hear listen! (Mk 4:22–23)

Praying with Scripture requires that we take the time to pause and clear the snow that has fallen on the once fertile ground. We must build a fire to warm ourselves by reading the text as if for the first time and letting the Spirit enkindle in us the flame of love. Then we will be led beyond the familiar story we have heard so many times into the realm of the divine. Only as we quiet ourselves and let go of our daily tasks can we find the golden key that unlocks mysterious treasures. If we are to allow the words of Sacred Scripture to transform us, it is not enough to read the words; we must savor them. Just as we can only hear a spoken word when it reaches our ears, we can only hear the word of the Spirit when it reaches our hearts. It is not enough to build a fire to light up the meaning, we must feel the fire of the Spirit in our hearts.

Of course, it is easier to hold the words at arm's length, less dangerous, because then we are in control of what thoughts arise from the text. Then we can safely imagine what Jesus really meant or how his message would apply to our own lives, rather than taking the risk of listening with an open heart to what he is saying to us through the Holy Spirit today. If we choose to pray with Scripture, we not only play with fire, we swallow it! As it becomes an intimate part of us, we will know the exquisite warmth of love. With the disciples on the way to Emmaus, we will feel our hearts burning within us (Lk 24:32).

The words of Scripture can only be absorbed into our lives if we make room for them. Silence is the space that invites them; the trust and openness of a child welcome them. During the contemplative moment our adult mind stands aside lest it unwittingly inject its own patterned interpretation of the words and stifle the breath of the Spirit that whispers wisdom ever new.

> From this time forward
> I make you hear new things,
> hidden things that you have not known.
> They are created now, not long ago;
> before today you have never heard of them,
> so that you could not say,
> "I already knew them." (Is 48:6, 7)

If we have truly heard this promise, we cannot help but stop in wonder. The impact of the words will create in us a tingle of awe that fills us with anticipation or, perhaps, a dread of the unknown. If we simply read on, we have not absorbed the words but merely skimmed over the uneven surface of the letters. Or is it that we have imagined that we are only reading what Yahweh said once upon a time to Isaiah? The living words of Scripture carry a unique message for each person who reads them. If we read the sacred text only as a record of events of ages past, we are insulated from the wisdom hidden in it and deprived of the creative, generative power which it releases.

Those who say they do not pray with Scripture because they have not studied it and do not understand it, do not realize the difference between approaching Scripture prayerfully so that the Word may speak to them, and finding it necessary to decipher the text themselves. The light that emanates from the inspired words of Scripture is the warm light of the Spirit of God, and holds within it a power that leads us beyond our own limited capabilities to understand. Moses did not understand the burning bush, but he approached it reverently and openly. Thus he was able to hear Yahweh reveal himself. It was a transforming experience (Ex 3:1–6). Elijah did not know why he had been told to go to the mountaintop and wait, but once there he heard the voice of God (1 Kgs 19:12). Holding the flame of Sacred Scripture in our hands and listening to its pulsating message is also a transforming experience.

At this very moment God is creating for us new things, hidden and unknown, that are revealed in the words of Scripture, and Scripture does not stand in isolation from our lives. The multiple strands of our lives with their deeply felt but untold emotions, external events, and unknown futures are intimately entwined with the themes of Sacred Scripture. That is why the message of Scripture affects us so profoundly when we listen to it with an open heart.

The golden key to unlock the mysterious treasures of Scripture has been placed within our reach, but in order to grasp it we must first clear away our habitual ways of approaching the Word of God. Then in the warmth of the fire of the Holy Spirit we can slowly, gently turn the key in the lock to find the untold riches awaiting us.

> I will give you the treasures of darkness,
> and riches hidden in secret places. (Is 45:3)

> If you only knew....(Jn 4:10)

2

Searching
Longing for Divine Intimacy

The kingdom of heaven is like treasure hidden in a field
which someone found and hid;
then in his joy he goes and
sells all that he has
and buys that field.
Matthew 13:44

From the moment we are born and gasp for our first breath, we continue to cry out for the satisfaction of our basic needs, confused at times by our perception of what will fulfill them. Soon most of us are able to take for granted what is necessary for our survival, so we begin to desire the extras that will provide comfort and pleasure, success in our endeavors, and a measure of security in our lives. This desire, in turn, is fueled by a deeper longing, the innate need for relationships with others, for bonding and love. Yet even the satisfaction of all of these natural cravings is not enough; there remains an indescribable thirst for something that will fill the interior emptiness we experience.

This continual searching has its roots in a profound, existential longing for union with the divine, the source of our being, and that desire itself is a reflection of God's own longing for us which is imprinted on our hearts. In fact, the energy of our purest desire is the breath of the Spirit that holds us in existence. Sacred Scripture is the story of this search for union with our Creator, a search which begins so poignantly in the Book of Genesis.

We read that one day when Eve was walking in the garden delighting in its beauty, she came to the very center where there stood a magnificent tree, the tree of knowledge. It fascinated her because it was the only tree that she and Adam had been forbidden to touch. God had told them they would die if they ate of its fruit! Eve did not understand that the death would be a separation from their Creator, caused by their choosing their own will in preference to God's will, their desire for knowledge and power in preference to God's desire for union with them.

As she looked at the tree wondering how it was different from the rest, a serpent spoke to her saying, "You will not die; for God knows that when you eat of it your eyes will be opened and you will be like God, knowing good and evil" (Gn 3:4–5). Eve thought about that, and, concluding that the fruit would make her wise, she ate some and shared it with her husband who was with her. This marks the first step in humankind's search for more, a search which was to lead us on a circuitous route to the divine. "Then the eyes of both were opened, and they knew that they were naked; and they sewed fig leaves together and made loincloths for themselves" (Gn 3:7). In his book *Second Simplicity*, Bruno Barnhart writes:

> With the opening of their eyes,
> man and woman discover a naked reality:
> a world stripped of the grace of communion.
> This is an externalization of the interior break
> which expressed itself in the sinful act itself....
> Immediately the whole human reality is fissured:
> relationships which had been borne within
> the unitive sea of grace are broken,
> so that blame, guilt, is transferred instinctively
> from self to another:
> from man to woman, from woman to serpent.

The separation experienced by the man and the woman was a manifestation of the rift they had created between themselves and their God. This chasm created by the false search for wisdom could only be bridged by communion with divine wisdom in the person of Christ, the Word of God. Jesus made that communion possible once more at the banquet of the last supper which stands in dramatic contrast to the meal in the garden of Eden.

As Eve and Adam felt the first blush of shame and stood there in bewilderment, they heard God walking in the garden at the time of the evening breeze, and they hid themselves among the trees. God called out to them, "Where are you?" (Gn 3:9). That cry, "Where are you?" reverberates throughout the pages of Scripture and in our hearts. It echoes in the words of Yahweh to the prophets and in the cry of the prophets to the Israelites. In the psalms, the people gave expression to their own experience of separation:

> As a deer longs for flowing streams,
> so my soul longs for you, O God.
> My soul thirsts for God,
> for the living God...
> while people say to me continually,
> "Where is your God?" (Ps 42:1–3)

As we pray with the Hebrew Scriptures, we hear God's loving plea for our return to him. Then our own aching for intimate union with our God finds expression in the words we read, and we receive encouragement for our quest. For example, the words of Moses to the Israelites before they crossed the Jordan into the promised land might have been spoken to us. He told them, "From there you will seek the Lord your God, and you will find him if you search after him with all your heart and soul" (Dt 4:29).

In the New Testament the story reaches its dramatic climax as God sends his only Son to dwell among us and assume our human nature, that we might be intimately united with him, even sharing his divinity! But Jesus' claim to divinity was difficult for many of the Jews to accept, although Jesus spent his life trying to convince them. Even today Christians act as if Jesus' words are too good to be true. However, their faith can be strengthened by returning to the Old Testament prophecies, and by remembering Jesus' own teaching as recorded in the gospels and reiterated in the New Testament letters and in the Acts of the Apostles.

Throughout our lives, we continue our search for the fulfillment of our deepest desire. It is not that union with God has not already been granted to us through Jesus' death and resurrection, and our immersion into that mystery through baptism, but that we are too limited in this lifetime to contain it in its fullness. The pattern of our entire lives is a journey toward an ever greater realization of our participative union with God.

At times we can be like the mythical Nasrudin who was seen searching for something under a street lamp. His friend approached him and asked what he was looking for. Nasrudin replied distractedly, quite absorbed in his task, "I lost my key," and continued looking. His friend was concerned and said, "How did you lose it here under the street lamp?" He responded, "Oh, I didn't lose it here, I lost it over there under that tree." His puzzled friend asked, "Then why aren't you looking under the tree?" Nasrudin answered as if the answer were obvious, "I'm looking for it here because there is more light!"

It is so much easier to go on searching for a deeper relationship with God in comfortable places and familiar practices where we feel secure, rather than approach God on the paths that are not as well known to us. For example, we may read spiritual books but avoid Sacred Scripture because it seems too dark and obscure. The attainment of our desire requires a readiness to trust in the guidance of the Spirit and a total commitment we may not feel ready to make.

Scripture is holy ground in which the gift of wisdom that leads to intimate union with God lies hidden. If we approach it in the light of faith, with awe, reverence, and anticipation, we are led by the Spirit to the gem we are to unearth on that day, at that moment.

> Ask, and it will be given you;
> search, and you will find;
> knock, and the door will be opened for you.
> For everyone who asks receives,
> and everyone who searches finds,
> and for everyone who knocks,
> the door will be opened. (Mt 7:7–8)

That text is expanded in John's gospel in the last supper discourse when Jesus says, "Ask and you will receive, so that your joy may be complete" (Jn 16:24). He could not have been referring only to our plea for material things, for they can never bring us complete happiness. What do we really desire? Do we realize what we are asking for? It is only the Holy Spirit who can inflame our faith and inspire us to realize that the treasure of union with God has already been given to us and lies within our hearts. The inspired words of Sacred Scripture help us to recognize and rejoice in that gift. The paradox is that we must continue to search for the treasure even while we possess it.

Paul offers encouragement in his first letter to the Corinthians. He reminds them of the gift they have received in baptism, which is not only the incorporation into the divine life but also the wisdom that enables them to know that gift.

> For what human being knows what is truly human
> except the human spirit that is within?
> So also no one comprehends what is truly God's
> except the Spirit of God.
> Now we have received not the spirit of the world,
> but the Spirit that is from God,
> so that we may understand
> the gifts bestowed on us by God. (1 Cor 2:11–12)

Thus through the wisdom of the Spirit which we have received, we are gradually able to understand the depths of the scriptural message that leads us into an experience of intimacy with God who dwells within us. That wisdom teaches us how to listen to God's word with open hearts, trusting not in human discernment alone but also in the guidance of the Spirit.

Sometimes the words of Scripture lead us beyond rational thought, prudence, and common sense. After all, Jesus did say, "I thank you, Father, Lord of heaven and earth, because you have hidden these things from the wise and the intelligent and have revealed them to infants" (Mt 11:25). Then too, Paul reminds us that the gifts of God are foolishness to those who do not believe (1 Cor 2:14). We must be prepared for paradox as we pray with Scripture and grasp its message, a paradox that is the expression of a truth beyond our comprehension. We search for that which we already have so that we might realize that which we know. So searching for our treasure in the words of Scripture even as we hold the Word of God in our hearts calls for a delicate blending of rational and intuitive thought, a balance of reflection and waiting in silence. It is that delicate blend of movement and stillness, action and receptivity, knowing and not-knowing that opens us to an ever deeper insight into the scriptural wisdom.

As we move reverently and expectantly through the varied genres of Sacred Scripture, the words penetrate our consciousness and seep into our hearts. Our lives will be enriched by our deepening awareness of the gifts we have been given, so that while on the one hand we will search for the hidden treasure in the field of Scripture, on the other hand we will long to realize its presence in the holy ground of our own hearts. Then like the woman who searched her own house for the lost coin (Lk 15:8–10), we will be confident that the kingdom of God already lies within us and we will ask, "Lord that I may see"(Mk 10:51).

The light that guides us in our search is faith. While it is an unending search for the limitless riches that God has placed within our reach, it is never a fruitless seeking, for even the desire for God is a treasure. The very emptiness that entices us into the solitude of the wilderness is a longing for God and a growing awareness of a divine presence within us. The more we continue our search, the more vibrant the light of our faith.

The inspired words of Sacred Scripture carry the very breath of the Spirit of God that penetrates us and becomes one with us as we absorb the word in our prayerful reading. To pray with Scripture is to breathe the Spirit of God.

> Therefore set your desire on my words;
> long for them,
> and you will be instructed. (Wis 6:11)

I invite you to join me in my wandering through the fields of Scripture, in a spirit of attentive openness to God's word. You may be called by Sophia, the Spirit of wisdom, to pause along the way, to delight in a flower, to drink from a stream, to reflect on a particular passage. I encourage you to open your own Bible often to read the entire text that is introduced in the chapter, or to discover the context in which a quotation is embedded. The Spirit guides us and speaks to us in individual ways, to reveal to us what we are ready to hear. So as we begin each reflection together, be ready to wander off to your own secret place whenever the sacred wisdom touches your heart and calls your name. There sit down and listen.

The thoughts on these pages are meant to open pathways that lead into the silence of your own heart where you can rest in an awareness of God's presence. As I write, I too will often stop along the way and sit by a stream to listen to Sophia. Some of what I hear will be shared with you; some will be held in my heart. So let us begin.

3

A Playful Spirit

Lady Wisdom as Guide

The Lord created me
at the beginning of his work,
the first of his acts of long ago....
When he established the heavens,
I was there,
when he drew a circle on the face of the deep,
when he made firm the skies above...
then I was beside him, like a master worker;
and I was daily his delight,
rejoicing before him always,
rejoicing in his inhabited world
and delighting in the human race.
Proverbs 8:22–31

These words lend a note of joyful, lighthearted playfulness to our scriptural prayer, reminding us that spirituality need not be laden with seriousness. It is filled with the delight of communion with our loving God. So as we open the Bible to enter into a time of reflection and prayer, we step into the embrace of divine wisdom who delights in our presence and guides us to a deepening grasp of the divine joy which gave birth to creation.

Wisdom, personified as Sophia in the sapiential writings of the Old Testament, tells us, "I came forth from the mouth of the Most High, and covered the earth like a mist" (Sir 24:3). It is she who delights to be with us and rejoices in our world, but we must learn to recognize her voice which can be heard only in our hearts where faith resides. It is in her own words that we read the poetic description recorded for us in chapter 24 of the Book of Sirach in which she tells us of her works, her qualities, desires, and promises. We are assured of her presence as she invites us to enjoy her company, saying, "Come to me, you who desire me, and eat your fill of my fruits" (Sir 24:19). Praying with the Wisdom books of Scripture we can become more familiar with her ways and deepen our trust in her guidance.

There is a carefree joyfulness in the Spirit of Wisdom as she wanders playfully through the world, a joyfulness that sheds healing light on the pain and conflict we so often encounter. She was present in the beginning when "God saw everything that he had made, and indeed, it was very good" (Gn 1:31), and she is present still. St. Paul must have been filled with the contagion of her joy when he wrote to the Philippians, "Rejoice in the Lord always, again I will say, Rejoice" (Phil 4:4). The joy of true wisdom exuberantly permeates all of creation. "For wisdom is more mobile than any motion; because of her pureness she pervades and penetrates all things. For she is a breath of the power of God, and a pure emanation of the glory of the Almighty" (Wis 7:24–25). While her delight is unrestrained in natural beauty and form, in the human heart she waits shyly to be recognized. Now and then, however, she surprises us with synchronicities and amazing dreams, as if she could no longer contain her desire to be noticed and accepted as a part of our lives.

I pay close attention to my dreams. Sometimes there is one that intrigues me because of its unusual quality, so I play with the dream image just as it played with me. Once I dreamed that I saw an elephant standing in the middle of a field. It was raining hard, so I ran out and stood under the elephant for shelter. Another time I heard one sentence in a dream, "Read the story of the goddess and the hare seven times and then you will receive the important message." Puzzled, I wondered about the symbolism of elephants and hares. My consequent search led me to mythology and fables, as well as to factual accounts of their habits. That helped me decipher the symbolic meaning of my dreams in which I discovered a significant spiritual meaning and learned more about myself. Along the way I laughed at the way pictures and figurines of elephants and hares appeared everywhere I turned. I'm still not sure of the full meaning of those symbols in my dreams, but I know that I received valuable insights and inspiration that have enriched my spiritual life. I can only wonder if the Spirit of wisdom was playing a game with me.

Scripture is replete with wisdom, and even there we often detect a playful tone in the midst of a serious lesson. For example, the proverbs frequently carry a note of humor along with their wisdom: "A slip on the pavement is better than a slip of the tongue" (Sir 20:18); "The lazy person buries a hand in the dish, and is too tired to bring it back to the mouth" (Prv 26:15). On the other hand, the poetic language of the psalms displays the graceful artistry of wisdom as she inspired the psalmists to use the beauty of nature to form their metaphors of praise.

The pastures of the wilderness overflow,
the hills gird themselves with joy,
the meadows clothe themselves with flocks,
the valleys deck themselves with grain,
they shout and sing together for joy. (Ps 65:12–13)

Jesus himself often said things in a way that would catch his listener's attention, using hyperbole, paradox, and simile. He frequently answered questions indirectly by telling a parable that seemed more like a riddle than a response to the question, and left his listeners pondering his meaning. Once when he was invited to a meal at the house of one of the leaders of the Pharisees, he noticed how the guests chose the places of honor. Rather than rebuke them, he told a story about those who are invited to a wedding banquet, and he drew a lesson from that. Later he approached the one who invited him and said, "When you give a luncheon or a dinner, do not invite your friends or your brothers or your relatives or rich neighbors..."(Lk 14:12). That startling piece of advice must have made the host stop and listen to what Jesus had to say! What could he possibly mean?

Jesus continued by telling one of the guests the story about the people invited to a banquet who all gave excuses for not attending (Lk

14:15-24). Read that chapter and, as you notice the irony and paradox of the familiar stories, notice, too, how artfully Jesus avoided directly criticizing his hosts. Instead, he made up parables that puzzled his listeners a bit but got his point across. It was a method of teaching that demonstrated his sense of humor, as well as his wisdom. Once we become aware of the poetry, images, and infinite beauty of scriptural writing, it loses its heavy tone and becomes an enticing entry into the wisdom of the Holy Spirit, even in the most serious of passages.

Stories embody a feminine, earthy quality that evades an analytical approach. That is why Jesus' parables are often hard to understand. We expect them to follow a logical line of thinking and are, therefore, completely perplexed when the ending is turned upside down. It may be the perfect opposite of what we expected! Their truth can only be discovered by joining the game and being caught up in the energy of the play. Once we become part of the story we are affected by its spell in a way that we may not be able to put into words. We simply experience the wisdom much as we experience the beauty and symmetry of a symphony or a work of abstract art.

Jesus delighted in using comparisons and caricatures that startled his listeners. With his words he often paints a picture or creates a cartoon that captures the attention of those he is trying to reach and is imprinted on their memories. For example, instead of telling people to stop trying to impress others with their generosity, he says, "So whenever you give alms, do not sound a trumpet before you, as the hypocrites do in the synagogues and in the streets, so that they may be praised by others" (Mt 6:2). That must have amused those whose guilt did not make them defensive! Another time he chides the scribes and Pharisees for tithing mint, dill, and cumin while neglecting more important things, such as justice, mercy, and faith. Then he almost shouts, "You blind guides! You strain out a gnat but swallow a camel!" (Mt 23:23-24). Jesus had a fertile imagination!

Holy Wisdom, known in Greek as Hagia Sophia, imbues our journeying through Scripture with a subtle inspiration that slips silently into our thoughts. As we come to recognize her presence, we relax, trusting that she will guide our reflections. Yet if we are to learn to know her, we still must remind ourselves to move slowly and attentively through the sacred words, for she has a way of wanting us to search for her and to watch for her. In fact, she tells us, "Happy is the one who listens to me, watching daily at my gates, waiting beside my doors. For whoever finds me finds life and obtains favor from the Lord" (Prv 8:34–35).

Why, then, if she desires to be found, does she seem so elusive? In the Book of Proverbs, the author describes Sophia with such passionate language that he sounds almost frustrated as he asks us, "Does not wisdom call, and does not understanding raise her voice?" (Prv 8:1). He seems to say, "Why can't you hear her; why can't you find her?"

Perhaps we are not pausing frequently enough in our reading to watch for her, or perhaps we are forgetting that she often speaks through intuition, inspiration, or an indescribable feeling that John of the Cross once described as "un no-sé-que," "an I-don't-know-what." The very seriousness of purpose with which we approach Sacred Scripture can cause us to depend too heavily on our own knowledge and wisdom, which, if carried to an extreme, can prevent us from receiving the insights of the wisdom that comes to us through the Holy Spirit.

In the Jerusalem Bible translation of the text quoted at the beginning of this chapter, we are offered a slightly different image of Lady Wisdom's role in creation. Rather than being told that she was with Yahweh rejoicing before him as he marked out the foundations of the earth, we read that she was "ever at play in his presence, at play everywhere in the world." Sophia is still playing everywhere, delighting to be with us, teasing, inviting, cajoling us to join her. "I love those who love me, and those who seek me diligently find me" (Prv 8:17). So let us enter into the childlike spirit of playfulness and simplicity, that we may search for her with confidence, forgetting for a moment the seriousness of our search, because that very intensity may blind us to the signs of her presence. She can appear in a multitude of guises, in exquisite natural beauty, in the innocence of a child, in intuitions and in humor, but it is in Sacred Scripture, the Word of God, that she is especially present. "For she is a reflection of eternal light, a spotless mirror of the working of God, and an image of his goodness" (Wis 7:26).

Through the incarnation of the Word of God, Holy Wisdom, who played before God and delighted in the human race, is present to us even more intimately than she was present to the people of the Old Testament times, because Jesus is the wisdom of the Father spoken in his Word. Paul refers to him as "the power of God and the wisdom of God" (1 Cor 1:24). This bond between wisdom and Word is evident in the similarity between the description of wisdom in the Book of Proverbs quoted at the beginning of this chapter (Prv 8:22–31) and of the Word in the prologue of John's gospel:

> In the beginning was the Word,
> and the Word was with God.
> He was in the beginning with God.
> All things came into being through him,
> and without him not one thing came into being.
> He was in the world,
> and the world came into being through him;
> yet the world did not know him.
> He came to what was his own,
> and his own people did not accept him....
> And the Word became flesh and lived among us,
> and we have seen his glory,
> the glory as of a father's only son,
> full of grace and truth.
> From his fullness we have all received,
> grace upon grace.(Jn 1:1–3, 10–11, 14, 16)

The Word of God took on our flesh that through Baptism we might be drawn into the life of the Father, Son and Holy Spirit. Then at the Last Supper Jesus, resonating with the joy of his Spirit, promises to pour out his joy upon us saying, "I have said these things to you so that my joy may be in you, and that your joy may be complete" (Jn 15:11). That joy was so deep and overwhelming that he experienced it even the night before his crucifixion, when he repeated the promise of Wisdom, "I love those who love me" (Prv 8:17), saying, "They who have my commandments and keep them are those who love me; and those who love me will be loved by my Father, and I will love them and reveal myself to them" (Jn 14:21). Then Jesus went on to promise to send another Advocate to be with us forever, "the Spirit of truth" (Jn 15:26), whom we may think of as Sophia, Wisdom.

How easily we lose touch with that joyful Spirit who gives us the wisdom to delight in all of life, and even colors our perception of moments of suffering and pain in order to transform our relationship to them. We can suppress the workings of Lady Wisdom within our hearts by confining her within the structures of learning, logic, rational conceptual thought, and other workings of our left brain. While she is certainly present there, she longs to be set free to express also her feminine qualities of nurturance, intuition, creativity, and contemplation.

Playfulness is best demonstrated by children who have not yet learned to suppress their glee. Their minds are not yet filled with responsibilities, worries, and planning. These necessary aspects of the fabric of life will always be with the mature adult mind, but they can be held in check in order to free up space for quiet receptivity. If you have watched children at play, you have noticed the focused attention they give to whatever they are doing. They are able to set aside every other thought and enter another world, a world as real to them as the world in which they live. This ability to move into another space and time requires qualities of childlike trust and openness that make it possible for one to be completely attentive to the present moment. That attentiveness opens our heart to Sacred Wisdom who enriches us with her gifts of love, joy, and peace which Paul mentions as the fruits of the Spirit in his letter to the Galatians (Gal 5:22).

This childlike spirit of simplicity with which we can most easily delve into the words of Sacred Scripture, then, enables us to be more attentive to the present moment, trusting in the guidance of the Spirit, and moving into our inner world where we make contact with Sophia who is ever at play in our hearts, "at play everywhere in the world" (Prv 8:30-31).

> To fix one's thought on her is perfect understanding,
> and one who is vigilant on her account
> will soon be free from care,
> because she goes about seeking those worthy of her,
> and she graciously appears to them in their paths,
> and meets them in every thought. (Wis 6:15-16)

So, let us answer Lady Wisdom's call and meet her in the sacred words of Scripture. She who has been present in creation from the beginning, will lead us to the treasures enclosed in the text, and open our heart to receive her gifts.

> Search out and seek, and she will become known to you;
> and when you get hold of her, do not let her go.
> For at last you will find the rest she gives,
> and she will be changed into joy for you. (Sir 6:27–28)

4

With Open Eyes

Personal Insight

If you turn to him
with all your heart and with all your soul,
to do what is true before him,
then he will turn to you
and will no longer
hide his face from you.

Tobit 13:6

This is one of those soft, spring mornings when I hesitate to pick up a pen lest I break the spell of almost magical beauty that envelops me. My senses drink in the sights, sounds, and smells of the fog damp-ened forest as it absorbs the early light. Bird songs slide down the silky redwood branches, to float through the air while the butterflies caress the flowers. Streams of clear water splash in the fountain, teas-ing the windchimes to play, and the steady, ceaseless sound of the rocky creek down below supports the melodies of the day. A ruby crowned hummingbird just arrived to savor the celebration.

Is this what it is like to look upon the face of God? Must I only pause, be still, and open my eyes, ears, my whole being, to drink in God's lavish presence?

"How does one move through such a day?" I wonder. "Do not tamper with it," says my soul. "Allow it to unfold."

"That is so easy to say," I respond, "but it seems so fragile and yet there are things I must do." "Do them," whispers my soul, "but do not tamper with the day. Move gently through it and the Spirit will reveal herself to you, even as you occupy yourself with what you must do. Resist nothing, embrace each moment. Savor the day with tenderness."

There are special days like this one that are offered to awaken us to the uniqueness of every day. If we are attentive, and receive the gift, we gradually learn to see the beauty enfolded in each of our days, even the stormy, painful, and drab. For those who have eyes to see and ears to hear, miracles abound; they grow out of the earth and sail in from the cloudy sea. The dew that bejewels the early morning is content to go unnoticed; the loss belongs to those who miss the miracle.

As I sat there on the deck in a meditative mood, I reflected that many of these thoughts can also be applied to Sacred Scripture, for the infinite beauty of the divine is manifested both in nature and in the Word of God. In the book *Mysticism and the Eastern Church*, Nicholas Arseniev recounts that Anthony the Hermit once said to a visiting philosopher, "My book is the whole visible creation, and it lies open before me whenever I wish to read in it the words of God." So everywhere, the Spirit waits to reveal herself to us if we move gently and quietly enough to be aware of her presence. Yet sometimes, when looking for the lesson in a long story or in a psalm, we miss the wisdom of a single phrase, just as when gazing at the vast expanse of a landscape, we fail to hear the melodies of the birds or feel the ground beneath our feet.

This morning I opened my Bible at random to the poignant Book of Tobit, the story of a father who, suffering from blindness in his old age, cared deeply about his wife and son and sought to provide for them. I encourage you to read the story yourself, for it is written with consummate artistry and filled with suspense. Let me tell you only of Tobit's joy in suddenly, unexpectedly opening his eyes to see again the faces of his wife and his son and the startling beauty of the world. In that moment he must have perceived a depth of reality he had never before appreciated, because he saw everything anew, as if for the first time. He cried out a hymn of thanksgiving and wonder, praising Yahweh and assuring his friends, in the words quoted at the beginning of this chapter, that if they turned to God with all their heart and all their soul, they also would see the face of God.

As I read those words again this morning, I did not focus on Tobit and the miraculous recovery of his sight, nor did I reflect on my continuing need for metanoia. It was the words, "he will...no longer hide his face from you," that touched my heart directly, at that moment, amidst the glory of a spring morning. This morning, for a moment, I knew that my heart had caught a glimpse of the face of God not only in nature, but in the word of Scripture. It was the scriptural text that awakened me to my experience of God's presence, as a sudden, intuitive insight burst into my consciousness. This was the playful touch of Lady Wisdom, making me open my eyes to the wonders of God.

I have long been fascinated by references to "seeing the face of God," and I have struggled to grasp that promise, to understand its meaning. The face of God is to me any manifestation of his glory that draws me into greater intimacy with my God, a deeper awareness of the all-pervasive presence of the divine. Just as seeing the face of a human leads to recognition, a glimpse of the face of God is an interior experience of the unique divine person.

In the psalms there are repeated expressions of a longing to see the face of God:

> "Come," my heart says,
> "seek his face!"
> Your face, Lord, do I seek.
> Do not hide your face from me. (Ps 27:8–9)

So also, there are cries of gratitude that "he did not hide his face from me, but heard when I cried to him" (Ps 22:24).

In Christ the face of God has become visible in a new way, for Christ himself told us, "Whoever has seen me has seen the Father. How can you say, 'Show us the Father'?" (Jn 14:9). Then Paul speaks of the "glory of God in the face of Jesus Christ" (2 Cor 4:6). Even further, he tells us that "all of us, with unveiled faces, seeing the glory of the Lord as though reflected in a mirror, are being transformed into the same image" (2 Cor 3:18). In a fourteenth-century Provençal tract imbued with the spirit of Francis of Assisi, who saw the face of God in all of creation, as well as in the inspired words of Scripture which he followed so closely, we read, "in all beauty that is in created things, man should perceive and contemplate—'la cara resplandent de Ghesu Christ qui resplandis e ri ins la beutat de las creaturas'—the radiant countenance of Jesus Christ, which shines and smiles in the beauty of all things." (This tract is found in Arseniev's *Mysticism and the Eastern Church*.)

Our God is much more manifest to us than we realize. We become aware of God's presence when we look with the open eyes of faith, but sometimes we squint, only half looking, because God's radiance bewilders us, even while it charms us. The more often we open the eyes of our hearts and discern the presence of God, whether in natural beauty, in the purity of a child, in the sadness of a suffering woman, or in the words of Scripture, the easier it will become. We cannot look upon the face of God and live—at least not the same life we had been living before our eyes met God's captivating gaze.

The grace of seeing God in all that surrounds us is as awe-inspiring as the miracle that Tobit experienced when he opened his eyes and was able to see. It was that grace which was given to me for a moment this morning. I savored it and knew that it is always within my reach. Why am I so forgetful of its presence? Sophia playfully made one phrase from the scriptural passage that I read leap into my heart and awaken me to God's presence.

The inspired words of Scripture pulsate with God's breath. Impregnated with God's energies, they lie resting on the page ready to spring to life when absorbed by human consciousness. "Indeed the Word of God is living and active, sharper than any two-edged sword…" (Heb 4:12). So today, as the words mingle with my feelings and sensations, they participate in my life, giving birth to thoughts and deep insights that arise as a fruit of that intimate encounter. These fruits are unique to that moment of union.

The Word of God is not sterile and static, spoken with one intent, frozen in a moment in time. It shares the paradoxical, unchanging dynamism of the Divine. Thus the words of Scripture carry infinite potential, endless meanings beyond the literal, historic context out of which they were first brought to life; they are weighted with metaphor, symbols, and images that enfold untold riches.

What the words of Tobit say to me as they resonate in my heart today lies not at the literal level, conforming to the meaning given to them by Tobit. They are spoken again to me, framed in the circumstances of this spring morning in the forest garden, reminding me to see God manifested in the vibrant colors, reflected in the clear, running water of the copper fountain, revealed in the softness of the musical tones of the chimes, to see God's faithfulness in the strength of the tall, straight redwoods, and her tenderness in the gentle touch of the butterflies.

No, I did not name these facets of God's presence as I quietly experienced God in the beauty of the morning. Names were not necessary, they would have fragmented the contemplative encounter, splintered the moment of intimacy. I struggle now to express in words what I have seen with the eyes of my heart, only to bring you into the experience. Words are limited in expressing profound truth, and infinite in the truths they can awaken in the reader. Listen to your heart as you read. Pause when you hear its whisper. The heart speaks in feelings, inner knowings, and a deep awareness more often than it speaks in words. We must learn to trust its wisdom.

This morning the exultant words of Tobit brought me to an experience of God as he reveals his presence in nature. For others, they may utter the challenge of returning to God with all their heart and soul, and the promise that God will then hide his face from them no longer. Someone else, yearning for solace in the midst of desolation, may realize that she has not behaved honestly before her God but has worshiped with a hypocritical spirit, content with the outward forms visible to others. That is the dynamic work of the infinite, creative spirit of divine Wisdom. She whispers to each of us personally.

The words "vision" and "insight" are closely related. For example, when we understand another's explanation, we exclaim, "I see what you mean." So reading about the restoration of Tobit's external vision can easily transport us to the metaphorical level of the incident. As Tobit's sight was returned, he may have "seen" God with an insight, an inner vision that he had never before experienced, realizing his mercy, goodness and power. He truly recognized a manifestation of his God in a new way and cried out to others that they might return to God with all their heart and all their soul, and participate in the same miracle.

That grace is offered to us. God is waiting for us to look upon his face and be transformed. Perhaps we will find our inner vision cleared only a little at a time, as we are ready, just as the blind man healed by Jesus received his sight only gradually (Mk 8:22–25). Then, grateful for our God's wisdom, patience, and gentleness, we will slowly begin to see a new depth of reality in Scripture, in the world, in others, and, yes, in ourselves. As we penetrate to our own deepest center, the light of God's presence bursts forth and illuminates all that we see, even if only for a graced moment. We gradually learn to see reality bathed in that radiance.

Approaching the dynamic, living Word of God in Scripture, let us open the eyes of our heart and always be ready for surprises. We never know how the word will touch us, how it will clear our vision, what insights will be sparked. It may lead us to an intense intimacy with our God, or challenge us to action that seems beyond our strength; it may simply refresh us and strengthen our wavering hope. And, yes, it may speak to us in silence!

"How does one move through Sacred Scripture," I wonder. "Do not tamper with it," says my soul. "Allow it to unfold. Move gently through it and it will reveal itself to you. Resist nothing, embrace each word. Savor the words with tenderness."

If you turn to him...
then he will turn to you
and will no longer hide his face from you. (Tb 13:6)

5

The Persian Rug
Varied Patterns in Scripture

> In order to arrive at what you do not know
> You must go by a way which is the way of ignorance.
> In order to possess what you do not possess
> You must go by the way of dispossession.
> In order to arrive at what you are not
> You must go through the way in which you are not.
> *T.S. Eliot, "East Coker"*

The experience of reading Scripture can be similar to the exhilaration and absolute terror one feels on a roller coaster ride. Promises of glory are juxtaposed with reminders of the sufferings one must first endure, Genesis is followed by Exodus, the garden by the desert, the crucifixion by the resurrection. The disciples were promised the reward of a hundredfold, but also warned that this would not come about without persecutions (Mk 10:28–30).

Our own lives follow a similar pattern filled with joys, challenges, and hardships. So, in this chapter we will weave back and forth between life and Scripture in an effort to demonstrate the intimate relationship between the shape of Scripture and the configuration of life.

Neither life nor Scripture is one series of sufferings followed by an endless period of joy. Each is a complex blend of unexpected ups and downs, delights and depressions, dreams and despair that creates a mysterious, exquisite design we cannot even imagine. The whole encloses and manifests a quality of contrasting darkness and light. It is the darkness, the terror and loneliness that empty us so that we might be filled with the fullness of joy and light. As Thich Nhat Hanh says, if we never knew the pain of a toothache, we could not rejoice in the experience of non-toothache.

Jesus first taught his followers that he must undergo great suffering, be rejected by the elders, the chief priests and the scribes, be put to death, and, after three days, rise again, then he went on to describe the conditions of following him (Mk 8:31–38). All of this must have given the apostles reason to think twice about their decision! But then, Mark goes on to tell us that Jesus took Peter, James, and John with him up to a high mountain where they could be alone. "And he was transfigured before them, and his clothes became dazzling white, such as no one on earth could bleach them" (Mk 9:2–8). They were suddenly lifted from the depths of despair to the heights of confidence and excitement. Jesus knew that if they were to face the reality of the hardships of their calling, they must be strengthened by glimpses of what awaited them not only at the end of their journey, but at special moments along the way.

T.S. Eliot, echoing the words of John of the Cross in chapter 13 of *The Ascent of Mount Carmel*, reminds us that in order to arrive at what we do not know, possess what we do not possess, we, like the apostles, must be ready to go by the way of ignorance and of dispossession. That is the way of faith. We reach the peak of ecstasy only by climbing up through the cloud of unknowing; the dawn comes only after the dark night.

The key to being able to look with the eyes of faith through the darkness of suffering to the brightness that will follow is in being able to see the picture on the jigsaw puzzle box rather than only the piece of the puzzle that we hold in our hand. The paradoxical challenge is to remember to envision the whole of our life while living fully in the present.

This is paralleled in praying with Scripture. In order to enter deeply into a particular psalm, gospel passage, or any part of the sacred text, it is important to recall that each section of Scripture, just as each day of our life, forms only a part of the whole. Often we skip over unpleasant segments, rationalizing that we do not understand them or that they do not apply to us, rather than immersing ourselves in the difficulties and demands that challenge us and possibly make us feel uncomfortable. Choosing to pray with only certain selections from Scripture leaves us with a distorted image of both Scripture and the Christian life. We must be willing to sit with Jonah in the belly of the whale and stand with Mary and the others at the foot of the cross, or we may never savor the freedom of rebirth and resurrection. We will be caught at an in-between place of dull, routine, tepid spirituality.

It is easier to plunge into the heart of the text and listen to it attentively when we pause to remember that at the moment of our baptism we participated in the resurrection of Christ and that we are in the midst of eternal life now, immersed in God at this very moment. Christ's transfigured life is within us and around us waiting to be recognized, but we are so in the habit of seeing our life as a long line of separate moments, days, and years that move up and down with a roller coaster rhythm, that we are oblivious to the eternal moment of glory in which "we live and move and have our being" (Acts 17:28). Penetrating the heights and depths of the sacred words of Scripture, we encounter both ourselves and the inspired Word of God, and become more deeply aware of our participation in the divine life. The eyes of our hearts gradually open that we may see the "light [that] shines in the darkness" and illumines our life (Jn 1:5).

This is beautifully illustrated in Alice O. Howell's book, *The Dove in the Stone*, in which she tells of a time when she was five years old and her parents took her to visit a Turkish Bazaar in Istanbul. She was so fascinated by the hundreds of small shops and an endless array of sights and smells that she had never imagined, that she quickly became separated from her parents, each of them thinking that she was with the other. When she realized she was alone, panic set in. She ran up and down the labyrinthine alleys and finally stopped in front of a rug seller and burst into tears.

Fortunately, he was a kindly man who spoke English. He invited her into his shop to calm her by showing her the beautiful, richly colored rugs and carpets. Then he asked which was her favorite and why. Listen to the conversation in her own words.

Gently he directed me to the pattern in the carpet. "Supposing, little Alice, you were a fly walking on this carpet. What color would you think the world was if you were here?" "Blue," I said. "And here?" "Green." "And look at this big stretch!" "Red, dark red." I was calming down. "If you were that fly wouldn't you feel mixed up?" First this, then that, then that and this, and that and this again?" He said it very fast so I laughed. It must have been a good description of my own impression of life. "Now, do you know what a design is?" I nodded. "Tell me, what can the little fly do to make sense of all those different colors?" I thought hard, and he gave me a big hint. "What can it do that you cannot yet? Think what it is called..." "Fly!" I fairly shouted. "Right! Then he can see the design from another level. It makes sense then, doesn't it?" He caressed my cheek and said to me, "Do you think you can remember that?" I promised I would.

Then the old man took her by the hand and led her out to the street to ask the help of a policeman. As they approached him, Alice squealed with delight when she saw her mother across the street.

It is easier to fly above Scripture and see the whole design than to do so in our own lives, yet for some reason we resist both. We avoid spending much time with certain words of Jesus and applying them to ourselves, just as we may avoid going to the dentist. Both experiences can be unpleasant. We are quite ready to assure someone else that going to the dentist can prevent future pain, or remind her that there are many rewards of a disciplined spiritual life, even though it may seem difficult. When we find ourselves standing on a black patch of the carpet, however, our overwhelming desire is to avoid it and to move to the light blue. Without a pattern of contrasting colors in our life and in our prayer, there would be no design, no exquisite pattern. Nor would there be any growth.

While applying this analogy of the variegated colors of the Persian rug to our lives as well as to our prayer with Sacred Scripture, and focusing on the perspective which is gained from viewing the horizontal aspect of the whole, it is important to remember that there is also another quality to the Word of God. Its intense vertical attraction thrusts us into an experience that is inaccessible to purely human understanding. The words of Scripture are full of the same Holy Spirit who dwells within us. Hence, they have the potential to draw us simultaneously into the unity of our own being and into the fullness of the divinity. Praying with Scripture, we may suddenly be plunged into the center of our very Self where we sense our unitive participation in the divine life. There are no words to describe that experience without distorting its authenticity. It is a moment in which we lose ourself while finding our true Self, and there finding God. While that occurrence may be fleeting and infrequent, it is a profound knowing which is unforgettable, and leaves us with a unquenchable thirst, with a deepening love. Once we have tasted the sweetness of the living waters that lie beneath the surface of the words, we are enticed to return again and again to Sacred Scripture, even though there will be many times when our prayer seems dry and empty.

The memory of one of these profound moments of interiority, or of a time when we were able to rise above the circumstances of our life—as well as difficult scriptural texts—and see them creating a beautiful design, will make us more patient in passing through the dark spaces. Neither Scripture nor life is monochromatic. The words of the sacred text are stories of the lives of real people. As such, they help us to see our own lives from a higher perspective, to avoid being discouraged by the mud puddle in which we are standing.

We read in the gospels (Mt 20:20–23) that one day the mother of the sons of Zebedee, James and John, went with them to talk with Jesus. He asked her, "'What do you want?' She said to him, 'Declare that these two sons of mine will sit, one at your right hand and one at your left, in your kingdom'." Jesus must have looked at her with compassion and understanding, for he had just told his followers of the terrible suffering he was about to endure. He realized that she was hearing only what she wanted to hear, being very selective in remembering his teaching, so he answered quietly, "You do not know what you are asking." Then he turned to her sons and asked if they had heard what he had told them. "Are you able to drink the cup that I am about to drink?" Of course, they replied, "We are able." Did they realize what they were saying, any more than their mother realized what she was asking?

We too have a tendency to ask to jump into the light blue or golden yellow of the carpet of our life, forgetting that we, like the fly, must go step by step. At times we can ascend to the heights and look down on the design we have already woven, and remember that we have made it through the rough spots into the reds and greens. That encourages us. It is important to see the meaning of variation in the design of our days, but then we must once again descend into the pattern and continue walking, just as Jesus walked his path through his earthly life. Because Sacred Scripture is the dynamic, living, divine Word, by holding it and gazing prayerfully into its radiant core we are strengthened to live the life we have been given, just as by sitting near a fire we are warmed.

We may find that sometimes the best way to handle the feeling of being stuck in a mud puddle is to wiggle our toes in the mud and feel the texture. Learning to feel our experience, whether it is mud, pain, or fear, whether it is physical or spiritual, enables us to move forward in our life and in our prayer. Avoidance, denial, and suppression only transform the mud into quicksand. Jesus was able to talk about his suffering because he allowed himself to feel and admit his fear and dread, and because he could see the light of the resurrection that would follow. He could put up with the criticism, misunderstanding, and accusations that so often confronted him because he did not try to escape them. Maybe he wiggled his toes in the mud and remembered the love and trust that his followers and so many of the townspeople felt for him. This helped him continue to walk the path through the black days and the bright days. Praying with the gospels enables us to follow our own path with faith and trust.

I once read the novel *Rayuela*, a Spanish word which means hopscotch, by the Latin American author Julio Cortázar. In the introduction he explains to the readers that they can read the novel from beginning to end, or they can follow a different pattern in the chapters, hopping from one to another while reading them in a specific order which he then lists. Whichever way is followed, the story is the same. He does not have to remind the readers that it is important not to skip any chapters. We are not in the habit of reading only selected chapters in a novel and expecting to understand the story, so, although I chose to play hopscotch and skip around in the novel, I eventually read every word. I must admit, I would not have persevered if I had not had to read it for a class assignment!

Scripture does not have to be read in any particular order, but it is important to be aware of the whole. Some parts can be difficult to understand, such as the accounts and details of the law in Numbers and Leviticus, if we are not familiar with the culture and times in which they were written. We sometimes resist the violent accounts of warfare in other historical books of the Hebrew Scriptures. They, too, reflect the values of the times during which they were written. The actions described and even praised in those narratives, however, also strongly disturb our sense of justice and of human rights. Our horror should serve to remind us of our place in the violence of our own times, even if our contribution to that violence is only that we look the other way. Some of the psalms even shock us either because of the linguistic devices of the Hebrew language, or because we forget that they were composed as poetry, so we read them literally. In the epistles as well as in the Old Testament writings, some of the references to women can make us want to close the book! They reflect the status of women at that time, and not the understanding of the equality of women and men which we see continuing to evolve even during our own lifetime.

All of these passages can serve to heighten our awareness of the forward movement of the Holy Spirit in the progression of human history. The important element in praying with any part of the sacred text is to enter into it with an open heart, remembering that, although it is the inspired Word of God, it was written by men who could not help but see life through the lens of their own cultural values. It is the fiery core of the words which touches our hearts today.

To paraphrase the words of John of the Cross, if we are to arrive at what we do not know, and possess today what we do not possess, we must be ready to let go of needing to know or of holding on to the security of control, and go through the way where we discover who we thought we were and who we really are. Yahweh's words encourage us to continue our search: "Walk only in the way that I command you, so that it may be well with you" (Jer 7:23).

In the words of Scripture we come into immediate contact with the Word of God, the Light of the World, who will shine on our path and guide us through each moment of our lives. Let us not be afraid to open our eyes and to follow.

6

Sacred Waiting
Rhythms of Scriptural Prayer

I wait for the Lord, my soul waits,
and in his word I hope;
my soul waits for the Lord
more than those who watch for the morning,
more than those who watch for the morning.
Psalm 130:5–6

One afternoon when I was living in a small Catalán town on the Costa Brava, I went to catch a commuter train to Barcelona, only to discover I had missed it and the next one would come in an hour. I sat down on the wooden bench in the sparse, dingy station to wait. After a few minutes had passed, I realized that although I had nothing to read and nothing to do, I did not mind waiting. That sounds like a rather simple realization, but it was so astonishing to me at the time that I have never forgotten that afternoon. During the preceding few months I had become accustomed to a different pace of life and let go of the intensity of the North American culture. I had lost the need to fill every minute with some productive activity.

It was also during that year that I found myself praying in a new way with a deeper, more contemplative rhythm. While it is true that I was only teaching a few hours a day and enjoyed more free time than I had as a high school principal in California, there was a different feel about time in Spain. The attitude of the people who lived a simpler lifestyle and their way of going about everyday activities, allowed one to be more attentive to whatever was happening in the present moment. I was immersed in a culture that values the gift of time itself more than the efficient use of every moment.

Our environment and pace of life have a profound impact on our spirituality and our prayer style. If our daily life is consumed by haste and tension, or by worry and illness, it becomes more difficult to create within ourselves islands of quiet which are conducive to prayer and meditation. Yet it is those interludes that provide the space in which we can feel the persistent yearning of our hearts for the nourishment of prayer. In order to find that inner quiet, we must momentarily step away from the pressures of our culture of expediency, efficiency, and competency, and step into an intense awareness of the divine presence which envelops us. While there are external aids to move into a period of silence, such as a special prayer space, a candle, or incense, these are not always necessary or available. If we cultivate the habit of focusing on the divine presence, the still point within our hearts may be found at any time even if we are surrounded by people and activity, whether it be at home, in a shopping mall, or in a doctor's waiting room.

That tranquil inner milieu engenders the willingness to be patient and to wait, qualities that are especially important in scriptural prayer, because the insight into the meaning of our reading does not always come immediately. Sacred waiting is a paradoxical experience of losing time as we embrace it, of expecting nothing as we receive everything, of being emptied as we are filled. With the psalmist we may say, "I wait for the Lord, my soul waits, and in his word I hope" (Ps 130:5).

An apparently empty period of quiet prayer is often a space of time pregnant with the fullness of life. Of course, there are occasions when we step aside from our daily preoccupations in an effort to be more conscious of God's presence and still fail to experience that fullness in our heart. Instead, we seem to remain in a sterile vacuum, devoid of feeling. This does not necessarily indicate a failure on our part, for the felt experience of the divine presence is a gift. All we can do is hold ourselves in readiness to receive it. Even when our eyes grow dim with waiting for our God (Ps 69:3), a glimmer of faith is enough to hold us in attentive silence. Faith is another gift that is too often taken for granted.

When we pray with the words of Scripture as our focus, it is especially important that we reserve periods of silent waiting in the midst of our reading and reflection, and be careful not to read too quickly or fill the whole time with our own thoughts. The words of Scripture must be given time to rest in our hearts and unfold their meaning just as flowers shyly reveal their beauty. They must not be continually encumbered by our expectations or efforts to force their secrets from them, for they hold the potency of divinity. Reflection on the words will, of course, bring us new insights, and we will usually begin by thinking about the text. Because our human limitations prevent us from exhausting the richness that lies hidden there, however, we turn to prayer, recognizing our weakness and pleading for assistance. Then we wait in silent openness.

Our own efforts, availability, and attentiveness are the gifts that we bring to scriptural prayer; in return, grace and wisdom are offered to us. We must "be like those who are waiting for their master to return from the wedding banquet, so that they may open the door for him as soon as he comes and knocks" (Lk 12:36). It is in silence that we will hear him knocking. "For God alone my soul waits in silence" (Ps 62:1).

This movement between active and passive prayer, so integral a factor in praying with Scripture, was schematically described by Guigo II, a Carthusian monk of the twelfth century. He spoke of four degrees of praying with Scripture, which he compares to four rungs on a ladder: *lectio, meditatio, oratio,* and *contemplatio,* that is, reading, meditation, prayer, and contemplation. This practice of *lectio divina*—the slow, meditative reading of Scripture or other spiritual writing—has always been encouraged among monastics, and later was taught to others. Guigo wrote, in the fashion of the time, with repeated analogies that clarified this approach to plumbing the depths of Scripture and discovering the indescribable wisdom which it holds.

Writing to another monk, Gervase, he first defined each step. Reading is the careful study of Scripture, a practice that is begun through the disciplined resolve of the individual. This is followed by meditating or reflecting on the text "to seek with the help of one's own reason for knowledge of hidden truth." During this phase, one begins to experience the rewards of one's efforts. Guigo then describes the prayer that follows as a natural movement of the heart in response to the truth the mind has perceived. In other words, the individual's desire for the treasure it has seen leads to an admission of his or her weakness and a plea for divine grace. At this point, experience or feeling predominates over the will, but individual intent is still involved. During contemplation "the mind is in some sort lifted up to God and held above itself, so that it tastes the joys of everlasting sweetness." Thus the last phase of this process is a pure gift which "inebriates the thirsting soul" with the joy of divine union.

One analogy which the Carthusian uses to describe these four steps of scriptural prayer is particularly graphic: reading puts food, such as a grape, into the mouth; meditation chews on it; prayer extracts its flavor; and contemplation tastes its sweetness. Notice the movement in which the proportion between active and passive or experiential prayer gradually changes.

In the conclusion of his letter to Gervase, Guigo cautions him not to expect the delights of contemplation to last. His soul should be ready "to descend gently and in due order to one or the other of the three degrees by which it made its ascent. Let it rest now in one, now in another as the circumstances of time and place suggest to its free choice." He closes his letter by asking his friend to remember him and pray for him if he is ever given the grace "to climb to the topmost rung of this ladder." That is an important reminder for us that the gift of contemplation is not always granted, nor are we to expect it, much less measure the quality of our prayer by it.

Due to our increasing familiarity with Eastern forms of prayer, in which meditation signifies a practice of sitting in silence and quieting the mind, we often use the word meditation to refer to contemplation. In Christianity, however, meditation has traditionally meant active reflection. During my years in the novitiate in the early fifties, when I was taught to meditate, I was introduced to the method of reading the scriptural text and thinking about it in order to apply its lessons to my own life. The meditation period was closed with a prayer for the strength to carry out the resolutions I had made. It was never suggested that I spend time sitting with the text in a contemplative mode. In fact, contemplative prayer was never mentioned.

That is not to imply, however, that the grace of contemplation was never given, simply that it was not named. Times have changed and the practice of a quiet, wordless form of prayer is again becoming better known among Catholics and other Christians. This is due in large part to the work of the Trappist monk Thomas Merton, whose writings opened the door to monastic forms of prayer, as well as to Eastern forms of spirituality. Other Trappists, such as Thomas Keating and Basil Pennington, placed contemplative prayer within a framework which could be easily taught, thus making it more accessible to all Christians. This particular approach was at first called "the prayer of the cloud," and later renamed "centering prayer," a change inspired by Merton's frequent reference to the movement into the center of one's self and into the center of God.

As we begin a period of lectio divina, let us always expect the power of the Spirit to be active in our hearts, "for we do not know how to pray as we ought, but that very Spirit intercedes with sighs too deep for words" (Rom 8:26).

At times the period of sacred waiting during prayer may seem unbearable, interminable, and fruitless. Our own efforts cannot calm our restless thoughts, especially when our frustration becomes yet another distraction. It may help to return to the text and then try again to reflect and to listen in silence, or patiently to repeat a word or phrase that caught our attention. Yet there are occasions when all of us find nothing but restlessness, distractions, and, perhaps, even drowsiness during a time reserved for attentive listening. The text we have been reading seems irrelevant and meaningless. It is all we can do to remain where we are and be available to the Spirit. That is enough. Such waiting is an expression of our faith and fidelity which will bear fruit at another time.

During this form of scriptural prayer, there will also be periods of consolation during which we are enticed by the Spirit to commit ourselves fully to the divine presence. Then we might say with Jeremiah,

You have seduced me, Yahweh,
and I have let myself be seduced;
you have overpowered me:
you were the stronger. (Jer 20:7, JB)

During these times, as the silence envelops us and we wait, an inexpressible yearning slowly fills our hearts. A profound desire for divine union holds us there, a desire for that which we already possess but do not experience. That yearning may be noticed as a feeling that emerges and takes our breath away, or simply as a tranquil awareness of the immanence of God. There are no words that can adequately describe it; it is a movement of love such as the psalmist struggled to portray in poetic form,

> As a deer longs for flowing streams,
> so my soul longs for you, O God.
> My soul thirsts for God,
> for the living God. (Ps 42:1, 2)

The very yearning for divine intimacy that we experience is like the shy deer itself. It is fleeting and free to come and go at will. It approaches when we least expect it, and holds us bound by its beauty. When it returns to the darkness of the forest, we can only wait quietly and patiently for its return, knowing it is there although we do not feel its presence.

A longing for God lies deep within human consciousness and can surprise us at unexpected times, even when we are in the midst of activity, for it is pure gift. I remember that one night as a teenager, when I was driving home with some friends after a football game, sitting in the back seat looking out the window, I was suddenly touched by a strong sense of love and desire for intimate union with God. That had never happened to me before. I was soon drawn back into the fun and excitement of the evening, but those moments left an imprint on my memory. Once we have experienced that yearning which is itself a presence, we will be attracted more easily to the quiet times of sacred waiting. Our thirst for the living God will not easily be quenched.

The movement of scriptural prayer might be compared to the rhythm of ocean waves breaking upon the shore and then receding into the depths. As we read, the words break open in our reflection and burst forth in prayer. Then as we pause and wait, the words disappear into silence deep in our hearts.

As we begin a period of lectio, we must always be prepared to linger with the Word of God, either to sit with it in the darkness without feeling its divine energy, or to be drawn into the fullness of its invisible power, where we allow ourselves to be seduced. Then the experience itself leaves us with an insatiable yearning for a deeper intimacy with Jesus, the divine Word. That yearning will invade our life and leave its mark on all that we do.

We will pray,

> O God, you are my God,
> I seek you,
> my soul thirsts for you;
> my flesh faints for you,
> as in a dry and weary land
> where there is no water.
> Because your steadfast love
> is better than life,
> my lips will praise you. (Ps 63:1, 3)

7

Window
to the Wind

Words as Barriers or Openings

The wind blows where it chooses,
and you hear the sound of it,
but you do not know where it comes from
or where it goes.
So it is with everyone who is born of the Spirit.

John 3:8

The windchimes have been singing for two weeks, touched by the fingers of the wind. Is their song one of joy or of sorrow? Is the wind massaging their slender bodies or striking them until they cry out in protest? Moving in cadence with the tall, swaying redwood trees and delicate tan oaks, perhaps they are neither happy nor sad but receptive. It is only we who judge and label events so that we might enjoy them or run and hide. There is no resistance in the chimes, no yearning for stillness. They move and rest in response to the urging of the air, totally attuned to whatever comes their way.

The wind creates its own path as it flows through the forest, gently or forcefully moving the trees from side to side, loosening the leaves and dry branches, telling them it is time to let go and fall to the ground, there to begin another stage of their journey. Since I have made my home in the midst of the forest, I have learned to watch the ways of the wind and listen to its whisper as it sweeps through the canyon. On stormy days I hear the wind coming even before I see the trees respond. It announces its arrival as if to say, "Prepare to bow before me and I will not harm you. If you are unbending and do not yield to my touch, you will splinter and fall."

Just as I sat down to write this afternoon I heard a loud popping sound and knew that a tree was about to fall. As I watched through the window, there was a sudden stillness, then with a slow, splintering sigh, a tall tan oak slowly slanted to the earth, gently eased to the ground by the other trees, breaking off some of their branches in its final bow. I was fascinated by the unexpected, synchronistic event. Why had the wind chosen that moment to speak to me? I listened to the thoughts that came to my heart, thoughts of the suddenness of death, the transience of life, the unceasing cycle of nature. The windchimes are still singing.

My thoughts turn again to the quote from the gospel of John about the wind. After describing to Nicodemus the unpredictable, independent qualities of the wind that seems to move ghost-like through the air, coming and going as it wishes, Jesus makes that cryptic remark, "So it is with everyone who is born of the Spirit" (Jn 3:8). Those words have always reminded me of a Zen koan for which there is no easy, rational explanation.

"So it is…." How is it? Is Jesus telling Nicodemus that those who receive the Spirit live in expectancy of the unpredictable movement of the Spirit in the depths of their hearts? Is he using that analogy to impress upon him and upon us that the presence of the Spirit, like the touch of the wind, cannot be seen but can only be known by its effects? Later, the night before he died, Jesus spoke more clearly to his disciples, telling them that the Spirit of truth abides in us and is with us (Jn 14:17). We, like the forest filled with the wind, are permeated by the Spirit who wants to shatter us out of our complacency, loosen our grasp on non-essentials, bring the rain to slake our thirst for the divine, and so elicit a grace-filled song of joy. Layer after layer of meaning can be released from these words of Jesus. It is not enough to think about them; they must be turned over and over in the heart.

In his book *Teach Us to Pray*, Andre Louf explains this way of praying with the word by referring to Cassian, the fifth-century monk,
who calls this the *volutatio cordis*, "the rocking of the heart, which rises
and falls like a ship, dipping in the swell of the Spirit; and so the heart
tumbles and turns the Word of God to and fro within it in order gradually to make it its own." Louf then goes on to remind the reader of
the metaphor used for this by the people of the Middle Ages: *rumi-
nari*, the chewing of the Word. He says, "One cannot help thinking of
some sleepy cows, settled down in the shade of a tree somewhere,
peacefully and incessantly chewing the cud."

These images bring me to a grasp of praying with Scripture which is
difficult to describe in other language. As I feel the gentle rising and
falling of the waves, or envision the cows peacefully lying in the pas-
ture, chewing their cud, without a care in the world, totally focused on
what they are doing, taking the time to digest their food, I get a sense
of what it means to stay with the words I have read. I allow the wind
of the Spirit to move through me as it will, never knowing where it
comes from, when it will come, or where it will lead me. Is that what
people do "who are born of the Spirit"? Does being born of the Spirit
imply a total receptivity to the touch of the breath of God, an awareness of its life-giving movement, and a trust in its invisible presence?

Insights like this allow us to relax into a period of prayer with the
sacred words of Scripture, realizing that the inspiration and insight we
receive do not depend upon our own efforts alone. Jesus said reassur-
ingly that "the Advocate, the Holy Spirit, whom the Father will send in
my name, will teach you everything, and remind you of all that I have
said to you" (Jn 14:26). Attentive to the guidance of the Spirit we will
see the beauty of God's revealed word unfold before us, and experience its embrace. The peace that fills us will overflow into our day and
be caught by those who come into our presence. It is true that the
Spirit of God, like the wind, can be a wild, demanding force, so that
some persons pull back from her words in fear. Yet one who is caught
up in the experience of love does not know fear, for the demands of
the Beloved are a delight. With faith and trust in God's love we can
yield to the Spirit's strength with no desire to resist her power.

I just took a break and walked out into the wind to look at the fallen tree. I was amazed to find that it had split apart down the center, leaving half the tree standing tall. I continued my walk picking up small branches to use for kindling. That interlude in the windy forest provided time for me to ruminate, to reflect on the difference between sitting in the house behind the window, safely watching the movement of the trees, and walking into the wind, feeling the cold penetrating my bones until I began to ache and returned to the warmth of my cabin.

If the wind of the Spirit is to penetrate my inner Self as I pray with Scripture, and cause me to ache, whether with longing love or with dread, I must open my heart to its touch. That is not always easy, even if it is always my intent. Immersing myself in scriptural prayer requires my full attention and a space in my busy day. Then, too, I do not know the form of the gifts the Spirit will bring. Challenges, self-knowledge, awareness of others' pain may be offered to me as well as a more profound sense of union with God. There may be gifts of desert times of dryness that alternate with delightful periods of consolation.

Sometimes scriptural passages will seem like clear panes of a closed window through which I can easily see the meaning of the words, but I cannot feel the movement of grace. The words appear to lie inert on the page. As I read, I am not aware of being nourished by the wisdom of the Holy Spirit, and I am unable to experience the solace or guidance for which I yearn. My customary understanding of the obvious meaning of the words is as far as I can go. No new insights or realizations emerge; only my faith reassures me that is enough for the moment.

At other times, as I pray with Scripture, the words spring open with new, deeper meaning that startles me like a rush of fresh air through an open window. Then I remain there prolonging and savoring the movement of grace, in awe of God's goodness.

For example, once while reading the well-known story of the Samaritan woman at the well, I was stopped by the words, "If you only knew what God is offering you" (Jn 4:10, JB). If you only knew....It was as if the words themselves had opened before me, releasing inexpressible mystery and wonder. That was a gift of the Spirit. The words I had read so many times were no longer a closed window through which the wind could not pass.

Another time, I came to Jesus' words, "I am the way, and the truth, and the life" (Jn 14:6). That particular statement had never meant much to me before. I appreciated it only intellectually, thinking that I understood its beauty. This time, however, I was captivated by the words, "I am the way." I focused on the word way, letting it tumble to and fro in my heart, not trying to analyze its meaning but fondling it. I was led beyond my usual image of a pathway which had always implied the dualistic concepts of following and imitating Jesus, and gradually realized or felt the unitive meaning in the word. Jesus is the way because I am in him and he is in me. In the words of Julian of Norwich, "Between God and the soul there is no between."

But the question remains, if the words of Scripture are windows to the wind of the Spirit, how does one open the windows, break open the words? One doesn't; the Holy Spirit does! All that is asked of us is that we sit before the window pane, looking through it with the eyes of faith as we reflect prayerfully on the words before us. Sometimes the window will be opened by grace. When it is not, we must be content with gazing through the clear glass at the beauty of the most apparent meaning of the words; that is enough. The Word of God enters our heart and rests there imparting unseen, unfelt grace.

> The wind blows where it chooses,
> and you hear the sound of it,
> but you do not know where it comes from
> or where it goes. (Jn 3:8)

Those who are born of the Spirit and who incarnate in their actions the grace they are given will always be nourished through the words of Sacred Scripture, even though the Spirit, like the wind, cannot be grasped for we are immersed in her life.

PART TWO

Touching the FIRE

Listening intently
as we touch the words of Scripture,
we discern the voice of Holy Wisdom
speaking from the we-know-not-where
in the mysterious caverns
of our being.

As we journey through
the stories, prayers, and parables,
she surprises us,
draws us to notice what we have not seen
before,
to hear meanings we had not expected,
and to marvel at God's ways
with the humble ones.

We move then in wordless silence
into the center of our heart,
there to experience
the divine presence.

1

Lend an Ear

Active Listening

We played the flute for you,
and you did not dance;
we wailed
and you did not weep.

Luke 7:32

Sometimes as I spend time with the words of Scripture, I think Sophia is playing games with me, no, not one game at a time but several. Sometimes just as I begin to dance to her music, I'm pulled within by a strong feeling of heaviness that seems to come out of nowhere, or an uneasiness blown in by the wind, or simply a pensive mood. I prefer dancing and singing to responding to those strong, inexplicable intuitions that pull me to an inner place of darkness, but so often it is only there that I eventually come to a sense of peace and, yes, joy.

But can I blame or, perhaps, thank the Spirit of wisdom for such unexpected feelings? Certainly not always, for they can be due to all sorts of influences—from the news a friend shares with me, to a change in the weather, to a flu bug. Yet it is often those very externals that lead me to a time of prayer that I would have skipped and to a level of insight that I might have missed. Sophia has a way of being ever present, playing and praying within us. There are moments when the inner music of the sacred words resounds with the lightness of a dance, and times when it carries a softer tone of longing or even of sorrow. "If you love to listen, you will gain knowledge, and if you pay attention, you will become wise" (Sir 6:33). Praying with Scripture calls for a readiness to respond to whatever gifts we are offered, and then to accept and reverence them in silence.

Jesus once became very impatient with the people of his time for their refusal to hear and receive the wisdom teachings of either John the Baptist or of himself. While John had come baptizing as he preached penance and repentance, we read in the fourth gospel that Jesus began his public life at a wedding feast by changing water into wine to save his friends from embarrassment. Continuing his ministry, he healed the sick, raised the dead, and preached a message of love.

Neither approach satisfied the people. They went on their way refusing to recognize the touch of God even as glittering sparks of wisdom were sprinkled on their paths. They trampled the seed sown in their own fields (Lk 8:5).

One can almost feel Jesus' exasperation and sadness as he says to them, "We played the flute for you, and you did not dance; we wailed and you did not weep" (Lk 7:32). Would he say the same to us? Our first reaction might be that we did not hear the flute, the call to rejoice, or we would have joined in the dance; that we did not hear the children crying or we certainly would have wept with them. But then, if we reflect long enough, we might begin to see scenes pass over the screen of our memories, and slowly realize the opportunities we have missed because we neglected our inner life, the times that we read Scripture without being attentive to the text, and suddenly realized that we had no idea what we had read. When I used to pray the psalms of the Office in Latin, I was told that as long as I moved my lips while reading them, I had satisfied my obligation. Perhaps that was true because I did not understand Latin, but now that I pray the Office in English, I still find myself so distracted at times that I have to read the psalm again to pray the words. I think most of us would admit that sometimes after hearing the first reading and gospel read at Mass, we could not repeat what they were about! "We played the flute for you, and you did not dance."

Sophia comes into our lives in such varied ways that there is no excuse for missing her completely. But let us focus now on her presence in the words of Sacred Scripture. So much of the wisdom embedded in the words seems puzzling, whether in the form of a parable, a psalm, an historical narrative of the Old Testament, or a teaching Jesus gave to the people. It can seem to apply only to specific circumstances of that time, or simply not to make any sense. While this may be true when one reads about the measurements of a temple to be built, or a detailed description of the booty collected after a victorious battle, that is not a valid excuse for putting aside the entire Bible. Although such accounts may not serve us well as openings to prayer, they do place revelation in an historical context, and they are important when we study the Old Testament Scriptures. The majority of the books of the Bible, however, provide an inexhaustible source of reflection.

In a previous chapter, "Sacred Waiting," I described lectio divina as a method which we may follow while praying with a scriptural text. It will be helpful now to give an example of how one may move through the four phases of lectio with a particular passage.

How, then, do we begin? We begin, if possible, by choosing an appropriate place for our prayer, one which will support our effort to move interiorly to a state of quiet attentiveness. We are content to be there, and try to be wholly present by letting go of other preoccupations. That is not to imply that we are so relaxed that we are not alert to the moment, to the text we have chosen, but that we are quietly receptive to the word of God. This is not a totally passive state, but one that is subtly charged with the energies of love, a love which may manifest itself simply as desire. It is faith and love which have drawn us to this moment, and they will sustain and inform our prayer.

Then we turn to lectio, the actual reading of the text we have chosen. We may first read the short passage for content, and then return to read it slowly, phrase by phrase. During the second reading I often notice words that I have skimmed over the first time, and which lend a unique quality to the meaning that now begins to emerge. To understand this difference, read the well-known account of the storm at sea in the sixth chapter of John's gospel. Then read it again slowly as it is written here.

When evening came,
his disciples went down to the sea,

got into a boat,
and started across the sea to Capernaum.
It was now dark,
and Jesus had not yet come to them.
The sea became rough
because a strong wind was blowing.
When they had rowed about three or four miles,
they saw Jesus
walking on the sea
and coming near the boat.
and they were terrified.
But he said to them,
"It is I;
do not be afraid."
Then they wanted to take him into the boat,
and immediately the boat reached the land
toward which they were going. (Jn 6:16–21)

After we have read this text, we may find it necessary to return to it repeatedly until one passage catches our attention or a definite insight emerges. At other times we may move easily into the second phase, meditatio, as certain words or thoughts strike a chord that resonates deep within us. We might find, for example, that we have read no more than the first few lines when we become aware of the fatigue and loneliness the disciples must have felt. They had been with Jesus all day, attending to the crowds of people, feeding them the loaves and fish, and now it was dark. They had waited for Jesus and he had not come. Suddenly our own loneliness surges up. We are not only lonely, but we long for the comfort and strength of Jesus' presence. He has not yet come. This sudden emotion may come as a surprise, "out of nowhere."

As we continue reading, our first realization colors our perception of the rest of the text. We, too, are rowing against a strong wind on a rough sea. Several issues are worrying us; we are tired and feel we can do no more. Because of our discouragement we do not even recognize Jesus' presence in our lives. Then we hear his voice, "I am here; don't be afraid." Those words may trigger in our thoughts a string of associations. I am. I am enough for you. I am the light; I am the way; I am the good shepherd. We need not spend time with each thought that comes to us, because all of them spiral around the one realization that now envelops us. In the midst of our loneliness we have not recognized Jesus or felt his presence, but he is here.

This knowing penetrates our heart, and we feel the warmth and pull of the energy field of the divine presence. It is like a flame that draws us deeply into contemplatio. We rest there without thoughts, captivated by the grace of communion with one whom we love. This experience may last only few moments, or may extend into the remainder of our time for prayer.

We may gently return to the words of the text, or we may find ourselves expressing our love and gratitude with the words of a prayer, thus moving from contemplation back to the third phase of scriptural prayer, oratio. The order in which we wander among the various phases of praying with the sacred words of Scripture will vary, and we will be guided by the Spirit. We will not always be led to contemplation, and may find that we are held in any of the phases of lectio, or that nothing seems to happen. What matters is that we have responded to the urging of the Spirit as we immersed ourselves in the biblical text.

I have described only one possible response to the above text. Everyone's experience of lectio divina will be unique, just as the individual's response one day will differ from his or her experience the next day. It is so important that we approach scriptural prayer without a rigid need to follow the rules. There are no rules; there are only suggestions meant to assist one in beginning the practice.

The grace we are given during meditation will not always fill our hearts with emotion and feelings. The fruit of our reading may be a quiet strengthening of our faith and our resolve to continue rowing in the rough sea, an inner knowing that Jesus is present and will reveal himself to us when it is time. We may find that we gradually become more aware of Jesus' presence than of our own fear. As that inner sense of presence clears our mind of all other concerns, we are content to sit in the fullness of emptiness, an emptiness unlike any other, one that is pregnant with divine presence.

An analogy comes to mind which may help to explain the interplay between our own efforts and the effects of grace during a period of scriptural prayer. Some years ago I was staying at a retreat center where there was a small lake complete with a rowboat. I have a weakness for rowboats and canoes, so I took the opportunity to row across the lake. It was a warm day and a gentle breeze was rippling the water, so I tucked the oars inside the boat and relaxed, watching the ducks approach to greet me, and enjoying the view of the wooded hills. I was enveloped in the peaceful beauty surrounding me and the movement of the water. Gradually I realized that the breeze had slowly moved me back to shore, so I took up the oars and once again rowed across the lake, tucked in the oars, and relaxed. This time I began noticing a large number of birds that always returned to the reeds at the edge of the lake close to twilight time. I repeated my trips back and forth across the clear water several times, alternating my own efforts in directing the boat with a quiet acceptance of wherever the breeze might lead me and whatever new sights and sounds might enter my awareness. As twilight came and I returned to shore, I was refreshed and had a new memory which would always be there to enjoy.

When we pray with a passage from Scripture, there is a certain amount of discipline and purposefulness involved. It is not the same as sitting in front of a television screen and waiting to be entertained. We must find the time, prepare ourselves, open the book, choose the passage, and read it attentively, reflecting on its meaning. We are actively involved in the process even as we are receptive to the movement of the Spirit within us. As our thoughts wander too far astray, we return to a second and a third reading, or focus on a particular phrase. The alternation of directing our thoughts and receiving insights and inspiration is continual and necessary. If we continue to row the boat, however, our own efforts will prevent our entering into quiet and listening to the sounds of the Spirit. We might even frighten away the ducks who want to approach and greet us.

There is always a temptation to stay with an analysis of the words and a hesitancy to trust in the guidance of the gentle breeze. Yet the presence of divine wisdom is all-pervasive and infinitely capable of inspiring us. "For God's foolishness is wiser than human wisdom, and God's weakness is stronger than human strength" (1 Cor 1:25).

So let us return now to the poignant passage about the children playing the flute or crying in the streets. Just as God's wisdom appears sometimes as foolishness and weakness, so also can it appear as joyful music or as loneliness that draws us into the divine presence. These are two sides of one coin, two integral aspects of the human experience. Lectio divina sometimes leads me into an experience of calmness and joy while at other times it triggers a deep sorrow. Just as the light that appears in the night sky illuminating the moon is a reflection of the light that appears in the day sky as the sun, so these various appearances of Lady Wisdom are one and the same. If we watch, we will recognize her.

If you love to listen you will gain knowledge,
and if you pay attention you will become wise. (Sir 6:33)

By listening equally to the music, the pain, the rain, and the bird song we will sometimes dance and sometimes weep, but we will always be graced with the transforming touch of God.

2

The Mystery of Wisdom

The Realm of the Infinite

But we speak God's wisdom,
secret and hidden,
which God decreed before the ages
for our glory.
None of the rulers of this age understood this;
for if they had, they would not have crucified
the Lord of glory.
But, as it is written,
"What no eye has seen, nor ear heard,
nor the human heart conceived,
what God has prepared for those who love him"—
these things God has revealed to us through the Spirit;
for the Spirit searches everything,
even the depths of God.
1 Corinthians 2:7–10

Delving into Sacred Scripture is an adventure into uncharted territory. No matter how many people have passed this way before us, no one has seen or heard exactly what lies in wait for us. The words are ever new and the revelations of the Spirit are boundless. The infinite, personal communications which lie within the text, cloaked by the limitations of language, are an inexhaustible source of wisdom. They lead us to an encounter with the Word of God, to a place where we touch the fiery core of mystery. Along the way we must pass through the transparency of the words in order to place ourselves in readiness for the gift of the Spirit that awaits us.

Although language is an instrument for sharing our deepest thoughts and feelings as well as mundane information and scientific facts, words are limited vehicles that carry infinite potential and bear the weight of both archetypal meanings and personal associations. "A rose is a rose," may be true at the literal, surface level, but may bring memories and emotions of love to one person who remembers the yellow roses in her bridal bouquet, or tears of sorrow to another who sees only the pink roses on her child's casket.

Deep within words are hidden endless waves of meaning: mystical, mythical, historical, and allegorical, to mention only a few. How then can one even begin to grasp the infinite word of God? One can only begin, over and over and over again, each time plunging more deeply into the reality.

The wisdom hidden within the framework of words streams through the cracks and spaces, and at times bursts forth in glorious light, the same light that permeates all of creation. It is the light of the Word of God, Jesus, the light of the world. When our contact with the words releases this hidden wisdom of God, we experience a moment of the glory planned for us before the ages began. It is an encounter with the infinite that leaves us without words to describe the inexpressible. It can only be held in our heart and savored.

In the first letter to the Corinthians, quoted at the opening of this chapter, Paul struggles to communicate his own encounter with the infinite, to share with his readers the marvels which no eye has seen, no ear has heard, and no one could imagine. His meaning lies obscured in the text, waiting for those who will return to it repeatedly, pondering and savoring the words until gradually, almost imperceptibly, they catch a glimpse of his message. The words and phrases must rest ·in our heart until they are ready to disclose their mystery. They must melt in the fire of our love and be absorbed into the depths of our being. Paul insistently assures us that God has revealed these truths to us through the Spirit (1 Cor 2:10). That is, it is not a teaching reserved for the scholars or even the saints. The wisdom of God is accessible to all of us.

Of course, Paul's letters can be difficult to understand, for they are not narratives that carry us in a linear fashion from one event to the next, but spiraling descriptions that lead us ever closer to the central core of his message. Some passages like the above cause us to struggle as much as Paul must have struggled as he searched for the words. Perhaps that is why he explains, "And we speak of these things in words not taught by human wisdom but taught by the Spirit, interpreting spiritual things to those who are spiritual" (1 Cor 2:13). That may be the clue to reading all of Paul's letters, and all of Scripture!

But what exactly did Paul mean? He tells us clearly that these things can only be understood by means of the Spirit. It is the Spirit who teaches us and who reveals to us the message we are meant to hear. The words of Sacred Scripture are not words of human wisdom but of the wisdom of the Spirit, and can only be grasped from a spiritual perspective, not a philosophical, analytical perspective, although that perspective certainly may serve as a foundation that opens our understanding. While it is true, therefore, that human reasoning alone only directs us on our quest and will not penetrate to the core of the hidden wisdom of God, we are not left helpless, because "Now we have received not the spirit of the world, but the Spirit that is from God, so that we may understand the gifts bestowed on us by God" (1 Cor 2:12). We must learn to listen to that teaching, a teaching of the heart, in a spiritual way, that is, a prayerful way.

When we rest in the presence of the Word and immerse ourselves in the luminosity of eternal wisdom, we come to know Christ in whom is the fullness of meaning. There we can approach Paul's encounter with the Word, not by simply knowing about it, but by knowing it, experiencing it, and tasting it.

There is a well-known anecdote that illustrates the different ways of knowing by comparing them to western and oriental approaches. It is said that if a person educated in the traditions of the western world wants to know all he can about a fish, he catches it, pulls it out of the water, and dissects it in order to study it in great detail and ana-lyze its inner workings. A person trained in the eastern culture would, on the other hand, put his head under water and watch the fish in its natural environment. The western way of knowing is to hold the object of knowledge at a distance and control it by acting upon it, while the oriental approach is to identify as closely as possible with the object—in a sense, to enter into it and experience it.

If we hope to know Scripture, it is essential that we approach it in both the western and eastern ways. But we must go beyond only read-ing the words, holding them at a safe distance; we must dare to touch them, to consume them. This unitive knowing of Scripture is more than understanding something other than ourselves in a dualistic mode; it implies an intimate identification with the object known. That intimacy is gained only through a prolonged contact that enables one to penetrate ever closer to the heart of the matter. There we begin to savor the warmth of the luminous wisdom which lies cloaked in the contours of the letters. We can only identify with something that becomes a part of us.

This process is not difficult; it requires no worldly expertise because, as Paul reminds us, these things do not spring from human wisdom. They can only be understood by means of the Spirit, that is, in a spiritual way. If we become discouraged in trying to understand a scriptural text, perhaps it is because we are dissecting it rather than living with it. If we want to know about air, we might read a descrip-tion of it in a scientific textbook, but we can know air only by breath-ing it, feeling the movement of a breeze, watching the ripples on a pond as the wind caresses its surface. It is a gentle, attentive process of getting to know air by experiencing its presence. In a very similar way we come to a unitive knowing of the Word of God through a gen-tle, attentive awareness of being one with him in the Spirit.

A personal identification with the divine Word is experienced as a gentle, progressive knowing. That is possible only because Christ identified himself with us, sharing our humanity, so that through baptism we might become one with him. This union is real yet incomplete, because it is never-ending. It is easy to read scriptural texts which remind us of our oneness with Christ, but the almost incredible weight of their significance can make them slide through our thoughts leaving no imprint. We need to return to them, pick them up, read them, and, yes, taste them until they become a part of us. We cannot understand them any more than we can grasp the air that we breathe, but both Scripture and air are essential for life. By internalizing the reality that is painted by the words, a personal identification with Christ can transform our vision of life.

Here we stand in the presence of the mystery of wisdom which is beyond the reach of human understanding, but not beyond the reach of human experience. Paul writes that he is teaching us "the things that no eye has seen and no ear has heard," for these are things that can be seen and heard only with the eyes and ears of the heart. This is a personal experience that is mysterious but no less palpable. Entering into the mystery of the realm of infinite wisdom is like learning to breathe under water. It transports us to a new level of existence, the life of the Word of God in whom "we live and move and have our being" (Acts 17:28). Once we are there, we know we have found our true home.

The all-pervasive presence of the wisdom of God cannot be confined in or conveyed by words alone. They are weak vehicles for meaning that can only carry truth in the context of a phrase, a sentence, or even a story that tells of a human experience. Words must lean on each other and collectively shed their light on the whole. Only then can their voice be heard. They play complex roles, say different things at different times. When it is anticipated, this very playfulness is enriching rather than confusing. When placed in context, words come alive and tug at our personal or collective memories, understanding, and intuition. It is there that meaning is born.

In his book, *The Dwelling Place of Wisdom*, Raimon Panikkar writes, "Wisdom resides in the spoken rather than the written word. Wisdom books are, by and large, collections of oral tradition that have been intensified and refined by the sieve of time." Every oral tradition is rich with figures of speech, similes, and metaphors in which earthy comparisons are often used to convey heartfelt emotions, because the rationality of academic speech is not adequate. For this reason, the words of Scripture must speak in our hearts and we must allow them to resonate in our lives. Only then will they disclose the concealed presence of God by transporting us into the divine mystery.

The oral tradition of wisdom stories can be heard in the parables and teachings of Jesus. The tale of the farmer who built an extra barn for his wheat; the metaphoric explanations Jesus used, "I am the vine; you are the branches" (Jn 15:5), "I am the bread of life" (Jn 6:35): they are all filled with images that touch the familiar experiences of his listeners. The language of both the Old and the New Testaments is a wisdom language, not an academic one. That is, its mysterious depth of meaning springs from the Spirit, is rooted in the lives of real people, and, therefore, bears fruit in our own daily experiences—if we give it time and attention.

Panikkar continues, "We are accustomed to reading words. We have almost stopped 'eating' words, and we are even less used to letting words become flesh and embodying them. That is so even though both similes originate in Christian Holy Scripture." So let us allow the words to penetrate us and become a part of us.

Theology, philosophy, and science all carry wisdom within them, but they are a human attempt to organize and categorize it, and thus run the danger of attempting to confine it. True wisdom will not be confined to one form of expression. It bursts forth in laughter and tears, in intuition and logic, in a violet and in a cascading waterfall. Wisdom lies in the depths of the earth and in the glimmering stars, in the tomes of university libraries and in children's story books. It is hidden only to those who try to force it into compartments and refuse to admit its omnipresence.

That is the paradox of the mystery of wisdom. It is always everywhere and never in one place. It can only be grasped with open hands and an open heart. Wisdom playfully takes us by surprise because its joy cannot be contained or controlled. All of creation is a manifestation of the infinite wisdom of God that is fully embodied in the person of Christ. We touch and absorb the Word of God each time we expose ourselves to that mysterious wisdom that plays on the pages of Sacred Scripture, for the very words of Scripture open out into the fullness of divinity.

Aware of the infinite expanse of this treasure of wisdom, Paul wrote,

I pray that you may have the power to comprehend,
with all the saints,
what is the breadth and length and height and depth,
and to know the love of Christ that surpasses knowledge,
so that you may be filled
with all the fullness of God. (Eph 3:18–19)

Paul prayed that we might be graced with the wisdom to open ourselves to Christ's love by knowing him. The knowledge beyond knowledge of which Paul speaks is a participation in the mystery of divine wisdom through which we realize within ourselves the fullness of God. This is the mystery into which we move as we prayerfully spend time with the words of Scripture:

"What no eye has seen,
nor ear heard,
nor the human heart conceived,
what God has prepared
for those who love him." (1 Cor 2:9)

3

Rain and Snow

The Immanence of God

For as the rain and the snow come down from heaven,
and do not return there
until they have watered the earth,
making it bring forth and sprout,
giving seed to the sower
and bread to the eater,
so shall my word be that goes out from my mouth;
it shall not return to me empty,
but it shall accomplish that which I purpose.
Isaiah 55:10–11

This morning, at the end of a long, dry summer, the first gentle rain of the fall season is refreshing the parched earth. As it permeates the soil, it brings promise of winter and hope of renewed life in the spring. Watching the rain, I am reminded of another time when I sat here entranced by snowflakes floating hesitantly through the red-wood branches, tracing lacy patterns on the needles and covering the earth with a virgin white carpet that invited footprints. Gently falling rain and snow both create a quiet atmosphere of peace that can easily lead one into a pensive, reflective mood.

But then thoughts of the other face of the weather, the unleashed fury of storms that tear the earth with raw power, began tumbling through my mind. Snow can arrive with the blinding force of a blizzard, paralyzing the usual patterns of life, just as hurricanes and tropical rains destroy and flood the cities and countryside. An invisible force seems to imbue them with a strength that no creature can repel or control. Yet as the storms pass and the waters recede, a stillness comes over the land, and once again new life slowly emerges from the terror and darkness.

The rain and snow are a double-edged sword, a two-sided coin. They are necessary for life on this planet, yet they must be harsh at times, and that very vehemence also brings the newness of life that follows death and destruction. They carry within them the potential for both blessing and curse, uniting the opposites into impetus for growth.

I have often wondered at this double aspect of the elements of our planet. Fire, wind, water, and even the ground itself that shudders in life-threatening earthquakes, all bear the forces needed to sustain life and the power to destroy. Can it be that destruction and creation, death and life, are dual aspects of one energy that weaves the web of the universe? "Very truly, I tell you, unless a grain of wheat falls into the earth and dies, it remains just a single grain; but if it dies, it bears much fruit" (Jn 12:24). There is transformative potential in death that lies unseen.

Even as we look back over our own life, we see that segments of our life, of our very self, had to be abandoned and even destroyed if we were to grow and mature. At the time, those deaths, leave-takings, and decisions were difficult and painful, but now we can see a change within ourselves that came as a direct result of those crucial moments. "For everything there is a season, and a time for every matter under heaven: a time to be born, and a time to die; a time to plant, and a time to pluck up what is planted; a time to kill, and a time to heal" (Eccl 3:1–3). I remember once writing a paper on Vicente Alexandre's poem, "La destrucción o el amor," in which he explored that very theme, that love unites the destructive and generative forces. As a college student I struggled with his meaning, but looking back on it now I understand it in a deeper sense.

In light of this reflection, it is somewhat unsettling that Isaiah compares the Word of God to the rain and snow that come down to nourish the earth and do not return until they accomplish their purpose. As long as our focus is on the soft rain of early fall the comparison is comforting, but as we consider the potential violence of the elements, the winter storms that leave destruction in their path, it becomes difficult to embrace the analogy. It is always more pleasant to think of the comforting, healing aspects of the Word of God, forgetting the strong, demanding tone in which that word can be spoken. It is, of course, possible to walk through the words of Scripture, carefully avoiding certain passages that we do not understand or that do not appeal to us. However, this selectivity may reflect a reluctance to open ourselves to the full spectrum of spirituality which incorporates challenge as well as consolation.

In the Old Testament the words of Yahweh were often manifested in thunder, fire, and prophecies of disaster, even though these were interspersed with expressions of love, promises of fidelity, and the reassuring refrain, "Do not be afraid." Then the Word became flesh and came to live among us. Gone were the thunder and pillars of fire. The signs and wonders now were healing the sick, feeding the hungry, and raising the dead. At the same time, however, threaded throughout Jesus' words of comfort were challenges to his followers to take up their cross and follow him, intimations of suffering that lay ahead, and, again, the phrase, "Do not be afraid." In the words of the letter to the Hebrews:

> Long ago God spoke to our ancestors
> in many and various ways by the prophets,
> but in these last days he has spoken to us by a Son,
> whom he appointed heir of all things,
> through whom he also created the worlds.
> He is the reflection of God's glory
> and the exact imprint of God's very being,
> and he sustains all things by his powerful word.
> (Heb 1:1-3)

The Old Testament word was often spoken in awe-inspiring settings that brought the Israelites to their knees and filled them with reverence for their all-powerful, transcendent God. Whether it was a command, a prophecy, or a word of consolation, it always offered a promise of life, a promise that usually required a reciprocal commitment requiring change, submission, or even death before the renewed life was experienced.

While the narratives of the Hebrew Scriptures often describe wars, violence, and famine in a way that repels us, it is important to remember that they reflect the values and morals of a culture far removed from ours. Yet we certainly cannot deny the unspeakable violence and suffering that pervade modern times in civil strife, starvation, hate crimes, world wars, and the nuclear threat. Only the mode of expressing violence and the manner of engaging in it have changed. Unless we read the stories of the Israelites from their perspective and experience, we cannot hope to understand their actions, much less their relationship to Yahweh. There is a message for us in these writings because, although they may not mirror the situations of our own lives, they are expressions of the human condition and, as such, touch our own experience even if in a symbolic mode.

Reading the narrative books such as Genesis and Exodus, the accounts of the prophets, or the psalms, we can enter into a deepening realization that our God is a faithful God, one who asks only in order to give in return. God asks that we obey so that we may be guided in the right path and be healed, fulfilled, comforted, and transformed.

The story of Naaman is one such example (2 Kgs 5:1–27). He, a respected army commander of the King of Aram, was struck with leprosy. After he had exhausted all possibilities of a healing in his own country, he was humble enough to follow the advice of his wife's Israelite servant girl and go to Israel to beg for help from one of the prophets. Once there he encountered a series of situations in which he was further stripped of his pride and sense of superiority, until he reluctantly submitted to a command of the prophet Elisha that seemed utterly ridiculous to him. Although he had expected the prophet to cure his disease personally by placing his hands over it, he was told by a messenger simply to immerse himself seven times in the muddy waters of the Jordan river! At first he indignantly refused, but his servants reminded him that if he had been asked to perform a difficult act, he would have done it. Admitting that, he complied with Elisha's request, and his soul as well as his body were cleansed. He emerged from the Jordan as one who saw himself in a new light and accepted Yahweh as his God.

Narratives such as this may remind us of our own hesitancy to believe, our pride, and a multitude of other qualities that may be a part of our own hubris. Thus, the account of another's struggle can awaken us to our own need for conversion. Then we, too, may figuratively immerse ourselves seven times in the waters of self-knowledge that we might be cleansed.

The New Testament, while filled with stories similar to Naaman's, lacks the violence of the earlier Scriptures and presents a different relationship between God and creation. Here the word is closer to our reality because it is cloaked in our humanity and spoken in human tones. While Jesus walked among the people as one of them, God's word no longer depended on an intermediary, an angel or a prophet; it no longer struck fear and trembling into the hearts of the hearer. Because of the incarnation of the Word of God, it became possible for humanity to participate in divine life, and so to enter into a new relationship with God. At the last supper Jesus told us, "You are my friends if you do what I command you. I do not call you servants any longer, because the servant does not know what the master is doing; but I have called you friends because I have made known to you everything that I have heard from my Father" (Jn 15:14, 15).

That possibility of intimacy with the Word of God made flesh created infinite potential in everyone's life, but even though Jesus became so accessible and walked among the people, they often did not recognize his presence. After all, he was no different from them. He came from Nazareth, a poor, country village. So when he spoke in the synagogue there one Sabbath, as was his custom, they were "amazed at the gracious words that came from his mouth. They said, 'Is not this Joseph's son?'" (Lk 4:22). Jesus must have been through other experiences like this, for he expected this reaction. "And he said, 'Truly I tell you, no prophet is accepted in the prophet's hometown'" (Lk 4:24). He was right. In their fury they drove him out of town and tried to hurl him off the cliff!

We, like the people of Nazareth, fail to recognize the Word of God in the ordinary events of our daily lives because he is one of us. Just as we do not see the air that we breathe; we are not aware of the blood coursing through our veins, or the messages leaping over the synapses of our nerves; so also we are oblivious to God's life flowing through us. It is so typical to take for granted what is nearest to us and forms the fiber of our being, because we cannot hold it at arm's length and observe it.

The very union of Jesus with us, with people we see, ironically, makes it more difficult to perceive his presence than it was for the Israelites to know Yahweh's presence in the thunder, because Jesus disappears into a unitive reality. He is one with us. The accessibility of the Word of God through the words of Scripture can lead to an indifference which, while not intentional, is nevertheless real. In fact, our very familiarity with the texts of Scripture can have a deadening effect on the dynamism of the words in our heart, unless we remind ourselves that they are ever new. If only, as we open the pages of the Bible, we could feel the awe of Moses as he took off his shoes to approach the burning bush and listen to the words of Yahweh. If only we could know the heartbeat of Mary when Gabriel told her the incarnate Word was within her. If only we could experience the astonishment of Naaman as he saw his body cleansed of leprosy. But we can!

As the rain and snow fall to the earth they meet a yearning receptivity. Though they may fall on a granite cliff or into a rushing stream, the ground eventually receives their life-giving nourishment. "The rain and snow come down from heaven, and do not return there until they have watered the earth" (Is 55:10). So also, the waters of the words of Scripture may at times fall on deaf ears or distracted minds. We may even turn away from an unwelcome passage, but if we continue to pray and allow the words to penetrate the parched soil of our hearts, they will bring forth renewed life.

We have been promised that the inspired words of Scripture will not return to God without fulfilling their purpose, but will "give seed to the sower and bread to the eater." They will satisfy our every need if only we receive them in faith.

4

Sitting By the Well

Unexpected Encounters

Jesus, tired out by his journey,
was sitting by the well.
It was about noon.
A Samaritan woman came to draw water,
and Jesus said to her,
"Give me a drink...."
The Samaritan woman said to him,
"How is it that you, a Jew,
ask a drink of me, a woman of Samaria?..."
"If you knew the gift of God...."
John 4:6–9

God communicates with each of us in diverse ways every day, through the glory of a sunny morning, a feeling of energy and good health, or even the heavy darkness of depression. Yet God's presence is so constant and so immediate that it is challenging to name. Somehow, we still wait for a feeling of devotion or an extraordinary event to nudge us and remind us of the divine, thus relegating God to certain predictable, obvious manifestations.

The seemingly incidental happenings that fill our lives are taken for granted, even though years later as we realize the long-term effects of a chance meeting one afternoon, or a book we read, we may refer to some of them as turning points in our lives. Then only are we aware that we were guided in a certain direction. Then only do we recognize the subtle urging of the Spirit that is with us always.

For example, I remember the afternoon that, on the spur of the moment, I chose Spanish as my college major rather than history as I had planned. I had no particularly good reason, I simply made the decision! That led me to experiences that I never would have imagined possible, and that certainly would not have been available had I majored in history. Among other things, I taught in Spain, ministered to Spanish-speaking people, received a fellowship for doctoral studies, and eventually was led through all of this to a contemplative life in solitude.

I do not remember that an angel visited me with the message that I should major in Spanish, nor did I receive a direct inspiration during prayer. But I do believe that the Spirit of God moves in the ordinary patterns of our lives, patterns so easily ascribed to chance or coincidence. That very fact calls us to a spirit of alert attentiveness so that we might be ready to notice and respond to the movement of grace that touches us so gently. How might our ability to recognize a divine inspiration be enhanced? We can increase our sensitivity to divine guidance by reflecting on the scriptural stories of people like us whose lives were deeply affected by their reaction to a rather ordinary circumstance.

In the next few chapters we will consider some examples of such incidents, for there are insights to be gained from the lives of those who have been guided by the Spirit. It is helpful to consider the qualities that made it possible for them to hear and respond to God's call, even though they may not have recognized it as such at the time. There are many such ostensibly chance occurrences recorded in Scripture.

Picture Rebekah, the daughter of Abraham's brother Nabor, carrying her water jar on her shoulder as she goes out late one afternoon on her usual errand to draw water from the well. A stranger, Abraham's servant, is waiting there, praying that he will recognize the woman destined to be Isaac's wife by the response she gives to his request for a drink of water. When he sees Rebekah approach, he runs to meet her and says, "'Please let me sip a little water from your jar.' 'Drink, my lord,' she said, and quickly lowered her jar upon her hand and gave him a drink. When she had finished giving him a drink, she said, 'I will draw for your camels also, until they have finished drinking.'" This was exactly what the stranger had prayed she would say, so he asked to spend the night in her father's house. The story evolves in a beautiful narrative and Rebekah agrees to return with Abraham's servant to become the wife of Isaac (Gn 24).

Could it have been mere coincidence that what Rebekah did and said corresponded exactly to the sign the servant had asked for? Was it Rebekah's own graciousness and ingenuous generosity that moved her to respond to the man with her customary hospitality? History, as well as individual lives, is shaped by such incidents. One can only surmise that Rebekah's sensitive nature and habitual desire to be of service to others prepared her to be an instrument of the divine plan, for the way we lead our lives greatly influences our receptivity to the inspiration of the Holy Spirit.

It was at the same well that Rebekah's son Jacob would later meet his wife Rachel. There is resonance of these meetings in John's gospel where we read another account of a significant meeting at this same well. One day Jesus was passing through Samaria and, tired by his journey, sat down by the well to rest. While he was there, waiting for his disciples to return from town where they had gone to get food, a Samaritan woman came to draw water at noon, an hour when a woman was not expected to go out alone. What ensues is one of the most detailed accounts of Jesus' long conversation with another person (Jn 4:1–42).

The woman was not acting according to the acceptable behavior of her time. As the story unfolds, however, we learn that she had often broken the rules of proper behavior in her life. At the well she encountered a solitary man, a Jew, who actually spoke to her, asking for a drink of water! She was astonished, but responded, asking, "How is it that you, a Jew, ask a drink of me, a woman of Samaria?" The woman was perplexed but did not refuse him. She kept the conversation open. It was then that Jesus commented, "If you only knew...." If you only knew who I am, what I can give you in return. She challenged him, and he began to reveal that he knew who she was and how she had lived; yet his offer was still there.

The exchange between them continued until she mentioned the

Messiah, and Jesus said, "I am he, the one who is speaking to you." Their eyes must have met at that instant of recognition with a look that was so powerful that she immediately left her water jar and ran back to the city to cry out to the people, "Come and see a man who told me everything I have ever done! He cannot be the Messiah, can he?" That phrase, "can he," spoke of hope, wonder, openness to the possibility, a yearning for it to be true. The people came and believed.

Read this story in John's gospel again and again. Listen to Jesus say to you, "If you only knew." Reflect on the qualities displayed by the Samaritan woman that enabled her to hear Jesus' words. These qualities might also enable us to be more open to the power of the word in Scripture, as well as to the incidents in our own lives that may seem insignificant at the time. She, first of all, took the risk of speaking to him. We might compare that to taking the risk of making an appointment to talk with someone, or even to spending some time in prayer, listening to Jesus. Then she asked for the living water which he had offered her, without realizing the profound meaning of that offer. In scriptural prayer, as in all forms of prayer, we must be willing to open ourselves to the action of the Spirit, without knowing how we may be changed or challenged. This stranger, a Jew, spoke the truth and told her things she had done which one would normally not admit to a passerby in a casual conversation. Her acceptance of his comments and her acknowledgment of her actions shows not only a certain humility and honesty but a readiness to change. It also indicates the power that emanates from the person of Jesus, for here we feel the presence of divinity. She realized that Jesus was no ordinary man.

When we open the Bible to read, it is as if we are going to the well to draw refreshing water to soothe our thirst. Like the Samaritan woman we have no idea of the living water that will be offered to us as we immerse ourselves in the text. Like her, we must be willing to forget our original purpose, to let go of what we had expected to learn from the words, to put down our water jar and listen. She must have looked at Jesus intently, and that contemplative gaze told her more than his actual words did, for it opened her heart. There was a certain resistance evident in the woman at the beginning, but she stayed there with him in spite of her doubts, captivated by his words. What was it that held her? It was more than the surface conversation, it was the person of Jesus. She felt the subtle movement of grace which she could receive only because of her attention, openness, and humility. At that moment she was ready, available, and thirsty.

We do not always feel ready at the time of prayer. It can be a struggle to drop our water jars and spend the time in apparently useless reflection. If our focus and intent is to be available and to rest in the presence of God, however, the words will penetrate our hearts and quench our thirst.

There are many more insights to be gained from meditating on this incident in the gospel. I will leave that to you so that you hear the personal message which the Spirit of wisdom will speak to you. As you read it, pause when certain phrases strike you. Allow those words to become a haunting refrain that runs through your heart. At any moment of our lives, whether in an apparently ordinary incident or in an attentive reading of Sacred Scripture, the Holy Spirit may touch our heart with unexpected grace. Unimagined consequences that will deeply affect our lives may flow from that experience.

As I was writing this chapter, I heard a knock on my door. It startled me because I live on a mountain road in a rather isolated area. People never come to my cabin unless I am expecting them and have unlocked the gate. I hesitantly opened the door and saw there two young men who had been trimming trees in the area to clear the electrical lines. I had passed them on the road and greeted them a few times, making sure they would not miss the trees on my property. Each time they seemed very grateful that I was friendly and could speak Spanish, since they did not speak English. Now one of them spoke and after asking how I was, very simply said that they had just finished lunch, but had no water. Would I give them some water to drink?

The synchronicity of the simple request astonished me! I gave them a pitcher of water and went out on the deck to talk with them for a few minutes about the forest, their work, and the expected storms. They left refreshed, and I had also been gifted. It was the gospel story in action. Each of us bears living water that we can share with others.

As they went back to their work, I stood there in wonderment, thinking of the simplicity of the incident and of the parallel between it and Jesus' meeting with the Samaritan woman. Those two men had unwittingly given me a living example of the gospel and awakened me to the reality of Jesus' presence within each one of us. Synchronicities have a way of exploding into our consciousness with a force that jolts us and clears our vision, making us look with new eyes at the present moment.

The Spirit, both in Scripture and in real life, touches us in a myriad of ways. We must always remain open to surprise. A fullness of mystery and potential lies within every moment, but an incident such as this one, because it was so ordinary, might have gone unnoticed if I had not just written the words of Jesus, "Give me a drink." That is the nature of the ordinary and familiar. We have only to be attentive, ready, and open to the possibility of wonder that may spring forth from the experience. Then our lives will be enriched and we will not thirst.

As we pray with Scripture we open ourselves to the unexpected. When we encounter the infinite wisdom of the word of God in our reading, we can pass by quickly, distracted by many things, oblivious of the divine presence; or we can pause to savor the living water and be refreshed.

5

One Thing Necessary

Dealing with Distractions

Martha welcomed Jesus into her home.
She had a sister named Mary,
who sat at the Lord's feet
and listened to what he was saying.
But Martha was distracted by her many tasks;
so she came to him and asked,
"Lord, do you not care that my sister
has left me to do all the work by myself
Tell her then to help me."
But the Lord answered her,
"Martha, Martha,
you are worried and distracted by many things;
there is need of only one thing.
Mary has chosen the better part,
which will not be taken away from her."
Luke 10:38–42

This is a multifaceted passage, replete with images that illuminate experiences common to everyone. Each time I read it I notice an emphasis that had been overshadowed by different thoughts during my other reflections on the text. Today I was intrigued by the word "distracted." Literally it means to be drawn away from one's original focus of attention or interest, or to be pulled in conflicting directions and thus to be unsettled or bewildered. Distracted reminds me of being "pulled off track." Martha's attention was certainly drawn away from Jesus by her concern for her guests and the work involved in offering hospitality. I doubt that there is anyone who has not experienced a similar problem during a time of praying with Scripture. We can begin with every good intention of being attentive to the presence of the Spirit in our heart and in the inspired words. Yet almost always there are moments of distraction when other thoughts, responsibilities, or worries come to mind. This is true in any form of prayer.

As an example, let us consider this incident in Martha's home. Let us enter into the words spoken as if we were hearing them for the first time, feeling Martha's tension as she tried to cope with the disappointment of being so close to Jesus and unable to attend to his presence.

It is easy to understand why Martha felt puzzled and frustrated. She had invited Jesus into her home in the hope of spending some time with him, but he did not travel alone. His disciples could hardly have been told to wait outside, and others may also have come into the house with him. So, there was Martha with a house full of guests, needing to prepare a meal or, at least, refreshments. She was truly being pulled in conflicting directions: the desire to be hospitable and her yearning to be quietly present to her friend, Jesus. She went to him asking for help. Her sister Mary should be serving all of these guests with her.

Martha's situation may reflect our own feeling when we yearn for a quiet time of prayer and are besieged either by people demanding our attention, by interruptions, or by our own thoughts reminding us of things we should be doing. We suddenly find ourselves pulled off track and either make an effort to return to our original intent or give up in frustration, planning to pray later.

When Martha asked Jesus to take her side, to her surprise he did not agree that Mary should help her. Instead, he recognized her feelings, yet pointed out that Mary was the one who had made the right choice. After all, Martha had invited him into her house, and then had given all of her attention to the others, responding to their needs, not his.

Perhaps he was trying to point out to her that he also wanted to visit with her, and that her choice to be concerned with other things was really motivated by her own unconscious habit of placing others' needs before her own. What would people have thought if she, too, had sat down and talked with Jesus? One of the most common reasons for someone not taking time for prayer and creating a space for it in her life is that she is too busy doing things for others. This seems to be a very charitable excuse, but it may not always be valid.

On the Enneagram schema, which describes nine basic personality types, this compulsion would point toward an excessive desire to respond to others, which is typical of personality type number Two. This desire to serve should be balanced by a recognition of one's true motivations and an acceptance of one's own needs. There are times when we must place ourselves first. Putting self first is not always selfish. We are urged to love our neighbor as ourselves.

On the other hand, Martha may have fit into the category of a number One, the perfectionist who must do all things perfectly, even when that causes her to set aside her own desires. This can be carried to such an extreme that the person does not realize she seldom attends to her own deepest yearnings.

Regardless of Martha's personality type, her intentions were good. She was a generous woman who invited Jesus into her home, not only to have time with him but to give him a respite from the crowds. The problem Jesus pointed out to her lay in her allowing herself to be distracted by tasks to be done and people to be served. Only one thing was necessary: her attentiveness to his presence in the midst of other legitimate concerns. In contrast, Mary was able to focus on Jesus' presence and be totally attentive to his words.

Scripture stories often present the extremes in order to capture our attention and spotlight the meaning of the situation described. Mary and Martha are described as being at opposite ends of the continuum. Where would we place ourselves on that continuum? Are we balanced and close to the center? Are we able to set aside sacred times of scriptural reflection and prayer in our busy day, as well as to integrate prayer with our activities so as to sanctify our lives?

Jesus' comment, "Mary has chosen the better part," does not necessarily imply that contemplation is superior to activity, as it is so often interpreted. The better part, the one thing necessary, is Jesus himself. Mary has chosen to give her attention to him; Martha has not. This implies nothing about the relative virtue of sitting at Jesus' feet or of serving others; of choosing a life of secluded contemplation or of responding to the needs of the poor by working in a soup kitchen; of praying or of working. The message here is that the best thing we can do in any situation is to love Jesus and to be attentive to his presence, no matter where we are or what we are doing. It is always possible to choose the better part by living in tune with God's presence, regardless of the external circumstances in which we find ourselves.

Scripture holds many levels of meaning and is ever new as we listen to the words. Some of the comments made by John Cassian in the fifth century apply to this theme equally well today. Writing about prayer, he comments that the Holy Spirit illuminates our thoughts in terms of our present needs and the circumstances of our lives at the time. He reminds us that

> The meaning of the words comes through to us not just by way of commentaries but by what we ourselves have gone through....The sacred words stir memories within us, memories of the daily attacks which we have endured and are enduring, the cost of our negligence or the profits of our zeal, the good things of providence and the deceits of the enemy, the slippery subtle tricks of memory, the blemishes of human frailty.

Then he goes on to say that, as we pray with Sacred Scripture, we soon see very clearly what is being said to us and can have a deeper understanding of it. Our prayer springs from a profound intuitive grasp of the meaning. We may then be led beyond any particular meaning into a moment in which we are caught up in the flow of grace. Cassian says, "It is a fiery outbreak, an indescribable thrust of the soul. Free of what is sensed and seen, ineffable in its groans and sighs, the soul pours itself out to God." Thus our reading and reflection may flow into prayer and contemplation.

Of course, it may seem that this can happen most easily when we pray as Mary chose to pray, sitting quietly at Jesus' feet, but there are times when we must assume the role of Martha. That can be done contemplatively also, but only if we are accustomed to gazing on Jesus in the depths of our heart during specific times of prayer. It is during those times that our soul is filled with the living water from the well of the Spirit of God so that our thirst may be quenched even in the midst of activities. In the gospel text, however, Martha was allowing herself to be consumed by her tasks and to be upset by the situation. This is indicated by Jesus' choice of words. He told her that she was distracted from her primary responsibility.

In the translation quoted above, we read that "Martha was distracted by her many tasks." Then Jesus said to her, "Martha, Martha, you are worried and distracted by many things." Notice that the word "distracted" is used twice. In the original Greek, different words are used in each case. The first word, *periespato* (which the gospel writer uses to describe Martha), does mean "distracted" or "overbusy." However, the word distracted placed on Jesus' lips is a translation of the Greek word *thorubaza*, which has a much stronger meaning. It actually means "troubled" or "disturbed." The other two New Testament passages in which it is used both refer to the feelings people experienced when someone had died.

For example, there was the occasion when Jairus begged Jesus to come and lay his hands on his daughter who was at the point of death. When Jesus arrived, the girl had already died, and the people were weeping and wailing loudly. He asked them, "Why do you make a commotion and weep?" (Mk 5:39). This is sometimes translated as "Why are you distressed and weeping?" "Making a commotion" and "being distressed" are translations of the same word Jesus used the second time to describe Martha's distraction. She was clearly more than distracted!

The other use of this word is in the Acts of the Apostles. It happened that one night Paul preached very late. A young man who was sitting by the window fell asleep and fell out the window to the ground three floors below. The people ran downstairs and picked him up, thinking he was dead. Paul went down also, "took him in his arms, and said, 'Do not be alarmed, for his life is in him'" (Acts

20:10). Paul meant something stronger than "Do not be distracted," when he told the people not to be alarmed; again we find the same Greek word. Here it is very evident that translations often do not fully convey the true meaning of Jesus' words. It can be helpful to compare various English translations of a text.

I think, therefore, that Jesus' words to Martha were meant not as a rebuke so much as an expression of concern. Martha had no reason to feel guilty about her efforts to serve her guests; only her inner disposition was out of focus. Her motives were good, and she was returning to Jesus with a simple plea for help. She yearned to be close to him, but her agitation prevented her from enjoying his presence. He answered her plea, but not as she had wished. If he had asked Mary to go help her, they might both have been distracted and troubled! That would only have made things worse. Instead, he gently reminded Martha, "there is need of only one thing." He was not referring to her elaborate food preparation. I tend to think he was referring to her distracted manner of going about her task. She was not doing it in a quiet, centered way in which she could have been focused on his presence. The one thing Martha needed was a focus on Jesus himself.

Praying with a passage like this one, we can listen for the meaning the words of Jesus have for each of us today. If we allow our activities to pull us off track or to consume us, if we cannot find time for prayer, or if, when we do pray, we are often distracted, we may be troubled, upset, and disturbed by our difficulty in focusing our attention on Jesus. We can then pray, "Jesus, don't you care? Please help me." He may answer, "It is enough. Only one thing is necessary. Your yearning for me is your prayer." As Cassian said, those words may "stir memories within us" that will open up volumes of meaning and realization. They may stir up a "fiery outbreak" of love and desire. Or they may lead us to a place of rest in which we know that the effort we have made, the desire that burns within us is enough. We may hear, "Be still, and know that I am God!" (Ps 46:10).

That is the time to stay with whatever feeling arises, to savor it and cherish it. Only one thing is necessary: Jesus himself.

6

Out of the Depths

In Weakness There Is Strength

Out of the depths
I cry to you, O Lord.
Lord, hear my voice!
Psalm 130:1–2

This painful cry of the psalmist is one of the most familiar refrains in Scripture. It echoes throughout the books of both Testaments with an insistence born of desperation, of a realization that human means have been exhausted. That experience comes at some time, usually repeatedly, into all human lives. It is a confrontation with the existential fact that human resources are limited, and that there is a point beyond which we are completely powerless.

That profound recognition brings us to a moment when we may choose to let ourselves be mired in hopelessness and turn in upon ourselves in bitterness. Or, we may look beyond ourselves and know as if for the first time that God is there, waiting for us to open our eyes and see him from a new perspective, from the depths of our weakness. The choice is ours even in our despair. We never lose the power to choose our response to life's circumstances, even if our only choices are either to give up or to cry out for help, admitting that we can do nothing. Total dependence on God paradoxically empowers us because it frees us from grasping for self-sufficiency. Dependence gives birth to an independence from our imagined need to prove our own power.

Scripture is replete with stories of women and men who found themselves in the depths, unable to rise above their pain and fear, unable to discover even a grain of hope in their hearts; in spite of all that, they cried out to their God. While reading their stories, we find ourselves in the center of an inexhaustible mystery that may also one day enter our own lives. Perhaps only a confrontation with one's own inability to change an external situation, to climb out of depression, or even to ease the grasp of fear, can open a person to a true expression of trust in God. Of course, these confrontations vary in their intensity. We do not always need to reach a point of complete desperation before being ready for a transforming encounter with God.

For example, there was a time many years ago when I was exhausted and could not find a way out of the situation which had deprived me of even the energy to pray. And yet, I did pray. I repeated the first lines of Psalm 40 as if they were my only lifeline. They come to me now in French as I prayed them then,

> J'esperais Yahvé d'un grand espoir,
> il s'est penché vers moi,
> il écouta mon cri.

"I waited patiently for the Lord; he inclined to me and heard my cry." The magnificent phrase, *d'un grand espoir,* ("with a great hope," or "with boundless trust"), resonated deeply with my feelings far better than the translation "patiently," which speaks to me of a more passive calmness and tranquility. I was neither patient nor tranquil! The hidden force of the French words rekindled my strength and kept me going until a resolution presented itself.

I had been an administrator of a successful, innovative high school for several years and enjoyed the work I was doing. I became increasingly aware, however, that my professional life was consuming my spiritual life. My first priority in entering religious life was to lead a prayerful life while serving others. Somehow that balance had to be restored. I asked to resign and to be allowed to return to teaching for a while. Permission was granted. Then, during that brief period between positions, I was asked to teach Spanish in a private American school in Spain. Again, almost incredibly, permission was granted, and I found myself living in an apartment on the Mediterranean coast and teaching only three hours a day! I now had time for prayer, solitary prayer. This was my first experience of contemplative prayer, and I did not even know what to call it. At times I wondered if I were really praying as I sat there in silence.

I spent three years there in Blanes, a small town north of Barcelona on the Costa Brava, and it was certainly a turning point in my life. Looking back at the rhythm of those years, I realize the graced potential of the mild desperation I had felt which led me to resign my administrative position, and so be open to the opportunities which presented themselves. The years in Spain opened the way to a deeper level of prayer and gave me time to discover a new relationship with God through Scripture.

Many circumstances can make us turn to prayer or open Scripture to search for guidance and solace. One of the strongest certainly is a pure bewilderment, a profound feeling of not knowing what to do next. The opportunity to face that blank future is a priceless, graced moment. At such times we are better able to hear the echoes resounding between the lines of a scriptural text because they touch our own feelings in unique way. Our emptiness and vulnerability create a profound need within us that moves us to listen with an open heart.

Prophets, saints, and ordinary people of all ages have known this moment, and have recognized its worth only after it has passed, leaving its mark on them. Listening to their stories helps us remember the frustration, fear, uncertainty, and even vague uneasiness that have crept into our own life, and the blessings that have flowed from our response. This remembrance enkindles our hope and trust as we look toward the future.

In this chapter we will recall incidents in the lives of three men whose stories are recounted in Hebrew Scriptures. Then, in the next chapter we will spend time with a few of the women whose intimate relationship with God grew out of their feminine experience. Mary, for example, was able to sing the praises of God exclaiming, "the Mighty One has done great things for me" (Lk 1:49). Yet she, unlike the men we will consider, had evidently not previously tasted total failure. This is typical of the women who were granted an intimate encounter with their God. We will explore that contrast as we listen to their stories, but first let us turn to the masculine experience.

Imagine Elijah, so fearful of Jezebel's threat to kill him after he had slaughtered the prophets of Baal, that he fled a day's journey into the wilderness. As he sat down under a broom tree, he prayed that he might die: "It is enough; now, O Lord, take away my life, for I am no better than my ancestors" (1 Kgs 19:4). Picture Job sitting among the ashes, covered with sores, having suffered the loss of family and possessions, so despondent that he prayed, "Why did I not die at birth, come forth from the womb and expire?" (Jb 3:11).

Spend a moment with Jonah who was chosen by God to preach repentance to the people of Nineveh. Instead he "set out to flee to Tarshish [modern-day Spain] from the presence of the Lord"(Jon 1:3), because he feared the consequences of what the Lord was asking of him. Soon he found himself the presumed cause of a terrible storm at sea. In despair and guilt, he told the sailors to pick him up and throw him into the sea to calm Yahweh's wrath. He had failed, and he saw no reason to continue living.

As we will see, each of these men was brought to a significant moment of grace and transformation, but only after having tasted the dregs of his frailty. Each was brought low that he might be raised to the heights of an encounter with God. Mary described this paradox in her words to her cousin Elizabeth: "He has brought down the powerful from their thrones, and lifted up the lowly; he has filled the hungry with good things, and sent the rich away empty" (Lk 1:52–53).

Let us begin with a visit to Jonah. He was thrown into the sea, fully expecting that this would be a final escape from his misery. "But the Lord provided a large fish to swallow up Jonah; and Jonah was in the belly of the fish three days and three nights" (Jon 1:17). Faced with the strange dilemma of being stuck once again in a situation from which he could not escape, he prayed as he had probably never prayed before. Consequently, the Lord told the fish to spit him out on dry land. And there stood Jonah, hearing once again God's request that he go to Nineveh and preach repentance to the people.

This time he listened with a heart wounded from a personal experience of despair. He had also realized the strength born of such a trial.

Jonah now had encountered the forgiveness and mercy of God. His faith had reached a new level, so he set off and shouted to the people, "Forty days more, and Nineveh shall be overthrown" (Jon 3:5). The people listened and changed their ways, and God forgave them.

This short, unfinished story is encouraging to us because it illustrates the vacillation so typical of those on the spiritual journey. Once we have gone through a challenging experience that has made us realize our need for God's help, we surface with new strength and new resolve. At some future time, however, we find ourselves once again weak and discouraged. Our life experiences spiral around a central core of faith that anchors us firmly through struggles that affect us physically, emotionally, and spiritually. We are gradually changed and brought closer to a more intense knowing, a knowing that is experiential rather than intellectual. As we come face to face with our weakness, our own truth, we come face to face with our God.

Each of these intimate encounters leaves a permanent mark on us. Jonah was not transformed into a perfect person by his first recognition of God's loving mercy, nor are we. The beauty of this story is God's understanding and patience. Jonah was a slow learner, but little by little he learned to know himself. Read his story and let it speak to you personally, for it sheds light on our own motivations. You may even discover that it mirrors some of the attitudes expressed in your own actions.

Job's story, on the other hand, presents a sharp contrast to Jonah's. Job is presented as a figure of unshakable constancy. An extremely successful man, blessed with a large family, wealth, and a strong relationship with his God, he was brought to a point of utter loneliness and failure. Although he wished that his misery might be taken from him by death, after listing his sufferings he was able to pray, "I know that my Redeemer lives...and after my skin has been thus destroyed, then in my flesh I shall see God, whom...my eyes shall behold, and not another" (Jb 19:25–27).

His faith rooted him so strongly that God found Job's fidelity unshaken throughout his sufferings. When God spoke to him, Job answered, "I had heard of you by the hearing of the ear, but now my eye sees you" (Jb 42:5). He realized that he now knew God in a new way, with the eyes of his heart which had been broken open to let in the divine light. God then blessed Job and gave him twice as much as before. He "blessed the latter days of Job more than his beginning" (Jb 42:12). This hundredfold which Job received did not consist solely of the external goods of family and possessions. Job had been granted an invisible reward engraved upon his heart and his memory. It was that gift which enhanced his perspective of life. He had fallen from good fortune into the depths of suffering and loss, and then been lifted to greater heights of wisdom and grace.

Our faith can be the strand of constancy that leads us through such difficult times. It is during those experiences that we learn to pray as we had never prayed before. Our prayer surprisingly becomes less desperately self-centered, until we find ourselves standing serenely on the divine ground, accepting the circumstances in which we find ourselves. We move from a repeated plea for help to an admission of our powerlessness and a simple reliance on God. A loving surrender becomes the keynote of our relationship with God. Somehow that silent surrender admits us to a space of inner peace that we did not expect. The feeling of desperation resolves into a living hope so that we can then pray, "I waited for my God who leaned toward me and heard my prayer." That time of true surrender opens the door to contemplation. It is a time when there is little we can do but trust, so we are drawn to sit quietly in the presence of our God.

Let us return now to Elijah whom we left sitting under the solitary broom tree in the wilderness, wishing he could die rather than face the future. Here was the great prophet who had accomplished an amazing feat in overcoming the prophets of Baal, reduced to a pitiful figure sitting alone in the desert. Elijah certainly did not feel patient and resigned; rather, he was exhausted, hungry, and desperate. He was terrified, bereft of hope, and could only wish to die. His experience is an example of how our physical condition can influence our spiritual state. He had no energy left for courage. An angel of the Lord brought him food and water twice, and he rested. Then, having received both physical and spiritual nourishment, he walked for forty days and forty nights to Mount Horeb. There he spent the night in a cave, safe from those who threatened his life.

The number forty in Scripture is symbolic of a long period of time, usually a period of intensive trial and difficulty. For example, at the end of the Israelites' forty years in the desert they came to the promised land; at the end of Jesus' forty days in the desert he began his public life. In our own lives we can remember similar times of development, suffering, and transition which led us to new vistas and challenges that we were able to face courageously.

Elijah woke up in his cave the next morning only to hear Yahweh asking him, "What are you doing here, Elijah?" He told Yahweh that he was fleeing for his life! Then, finally, the significant moment came. He was told, "Go out and stand on the mountain before the Lord, for the Lord is about to pass by" (1 Kgs 19:9–11). One last proof of his faith was asked of Elijah. He went out and stood there steadfastly through a wind so strong that it split the mountain and broke rocks into pieces. He stood there through an earthquake and a fire, but he did not find the Lord in any of these fierce manifestations. Suddenly there was "a sound of sheer silence" that filled Elijah with a vibrant awe. Recognizing then the presence of the Lord, he "wrapped his face in his mantle and went out and stood at the entrance of the cave," only to hear the same question, "What are you doing here, Elijah?" He gave the same answer as before, but with a deeper confidence and trust, for he had passed through a humbling, maturing process and been healed from a temporary weakness. He was now ready to receive instructions for the next step in his mission (1 Kgs 19:4–18). This episode reminds us of the healing power of silence which makes it possible for us to sense God's presence.

During this lengthy trial which brought Elijah to a more profound realization of his own powerlessness, he could not foresee the blessing he would receive, the unshakable conviction of Yahweh's presence and support that he would experience. He may have felt at times that he was running blindly into the wilderness, bereft of both human and divine assistance. We can understand the strong sense of total desperation that led him into the cave of his heart where he felt the terror of wind, earthquake, and fire. Only then, because he persevered, could he hear his God in the "sheer silence."

That phrase is one that translators have struggled to express in the vernacular. We have most often heard it translated as "a still, small voice," or, in the Jerusalem Bible, "the sound of a gentle breeze." In the Hebrew lexicon it is defined as "an articulate whisper." In this expression, which is an attempt to describe the sound of God, I have always felt the implication that the sound of God can only be heard interiorly. The voice of God is heard not with the senses that perceive external words or the clamor of the world, but with the intuition of a quiet, receptive heart.

Jonah, Job, and Elijah were each brought from the depth of suffering to a peak moment of readiness to listen. Through their struggles and bewilderment their eyes were opened to a fresh vision of reality that held them spellbound. The bonds that finally held them and quieted their own frantic efforts to understand, to solve their own dilemma, and to escape from their suffering, were humility, faith, acceptance, surrender, and trust. These seemingly constricting chains freed them to be true to themselves and to their God. The very emotions, sufferings, and fears that threaten to paralyze us can bring us to a deeper union with God. They free us to look within rather than search for answers where they cannot be found. Within we hear only a sheer silence that enfolds an articulate whisper, the voice of God asking, "Why are you here?" The answer is in the question.

While you pray with Sacred Scripture, notice the questions that arise in your own mind, as well as those in the text, for often there is a profound reason for your question. Following it to its source, you may come upon a truth, a grain of self-knowledge that had been hidden from your awareness until now. For example, in this episode of Elijah's life, you may hear the Spirit asking you, "Why are you here?" The question may lead you to ask yourself, "Why am I here?" You know the answer, but it may not be the first facile response that comes to mind. Wait in the silence, search more deeply.

Out of the depths you cry out to your God. From the depths of your heart you will hear his articulate whisper which holds a message only you can hear, spoken in the language only faith comprehends.

Out of the Shadows

Women of Courage

You who live in the shelter
of the Most High,
who abide in the shadow
of the Almighty,
will say to the Lord,
"My refuge and my fortress;
my God, in whom I trust."
Psalm 91:1–2

The heaviness of darkness gives birth to light, just as dry wood bursts into vibrant flame. So also, the experience of faith-filled waiting and patient acceptance engender strength and vitality. In parallel fashion, the stunning actions of women in Scripture seem to burst out of the shadows of anonymity and repression. Women emerge into a moment of history and set it afire, lighting up the darkness that lies over the scene, embodying the movement of the Spirit who sparks their courage.

At the beginning of the gospel of Luke, Mary is in the midst of a very routine day. She is startled by the appearance of the angel Gabriel and told that she will conceive and bear a son; she asks how this can be since she is a virgin. The angel explains that Mary will conceive through the power of God which will overshadow her. "The Holy Spirit will come upon you, and the power of the Most High will overshadow you" (Lk 1:35). From the depth of the shadow came the light of the world because Mary trusted in her God.

Even at the end of Jesus' life, it was the women who stood by his cross as "darkness came over the whole land" (Lk 23:44), who had the strength to bear his agony and the derision of the people who condemned him. Then, Jesus' resurrection from the dead is first revealed to a woman in the pre-dawn darkness. We are told, "Early on the first day of the week, while it was still dark, Mary Magdalene came to the tomb and saw that the stone had been removed from the tomb" (Jn 20:1). It was women who braved the shadows and darkness. It was there that they received their strength.

The stories of women play a central role in Jesus' life, for many of the significant actions and turning points in his ministry were initiated by them. For example, the transformation of water into wine at the wedding feast at Cana marks the initiation of his public ministry in John's gospel. Here it was his mother who urged him to take this step into the public spotlight (Jn 2:3).

It was his conversation with a woman who came to draw water at the well that led her to believe in him. She ran to tell the people of her Samaritan village, so that they also believed (Jn 4:4–42). That Samaritan woman certainly came forth from the darkness of a sinful life and was, perhaps, an outcast among her own people.

Later it was Mary and Martha who told Jesus of their brother Lazarus' illness, asking their friend to come to heal him. Jesus waited until Lazarus had died and was buried before he went to their assistance. But it was his raising of Lazarus from the grave that was the conclusive miracle which precipitated the events that led to his own crucifixion and death (Jn 11:1–53). So also, this miracle prefigured Jesus' own resurrection.

In the gospels we are told as much or more about individual women as we are about the twelve apostles who are most often referred to as a group. Women stood out as persons of remarkable strength, yet they are too often overlooked in scriptural reflection, even as they were during their lives. Observing these women in contrast to the men of the Scriptures, we see them emerging out of the shadows cast upon them by societal structures, obscurity thrown over them like a veil by the power wielded by men. Each of them appears as if out of nowhere, a determined, courageous person ready to act out of her own truth.

No prelude to this hidden strength is described for us in these incidents, whereas the stories of men such as Elijah, Job, Moses, Jacob, Peter, and Paul detail their struggles. These were men who showed remarkable courage after being brought low, perhaps because through that experience they learned to know their weakness and to realize that their strength was from God. Men were perceived as courageous, so their fear and frailty were dramatized and made clear as their stories were told to highlight the power of grace. Women, however, were assumed to be weak. The writers of the Hebrew Scriptures, as well as the evangelists, did not think it necessary to describe a condition that was taken for granted. Within the women of Scripture lay an unexpected determination that engendered a dynamic responsiveness to the Spirit.

Recall the occasion when Jesus multiplied the loaves and fishes to feed the multitude. The evangelist carefully impresses us with the magnitude of the miracle by telling us of the number of men who were present, without including the women. It was as if they were invisible, of such little importance that they did not deserve to be noticed (Mt 15:38). This omission captures the societal perception of women which is reflected in Scripture. It is important, however, to remember not only that their actions were circumscribed by the limitations of their cultural milieu, but also that, on the other hand, their presence was noted by the men who recorded the incidents in which they played a central part. The very fact that they were mentioned at key moments gives us an insight into the unforgettable poignancy of their actions.

So many times the presence of a woman in a gospel narrative breaks open the event, lifting it out of the ordinary and revealing a gem-like facet of the mystery of Jesus which might otherwise have lay hidden in the mundane overlay of the occasion. The meeting of a woman with Jesus frequently results in a manifestation of the Spirit and lays open an unexpected divine aspect of the person of the Messiah.

For example, there was the day when one of the Pharisees invited Jesus to come to his house for a meal. We can easily picture the men reclining at table, conversing about the events of the day, nothing out of the ordinary happening. Suddenly an uninvited woman, described as a sinner, appeared in the room and approached Jesus, carrying an alabaster jar of ointment. She said nothing, simply "stood behind him at his feet, weeping, and began to bathe his feet with her tears and to dry them with her hair. Then she continued kissing his feet and anointing them with the ointment" (Lk 7:38). This unleashed a torrent of controversy! The Pharisees accused Jesus of not being a prophet after all, for if he were, he would have known what kind of woman was anointing him and would not have allowed her to touch him. Jesus did not accept this lightly, but used the incident to expose the hypocrisy of the Pharisees and to praise the love the woman had shown him. He then turned to the woman, who had not fled the scene but had remained in her place at his side, and said to her, "Your sins are forgiven....Your faith has saved you; go in peace" (Lk 7:48, 50). Divine compassion burst forth from Jesus, revealing a truth not understood, much less accepted, by the Pharisees: he had the power to forgive sins!

The entrance of that woman into the banquet room was a startling event that turned the tables on the self-important Pharisees and some of the other guests. It exposed their failure to believe in Jesus' words, and highlighted the contrast between the hardness of their hearts and the faith of the woman. But what had transpired in the heart of that woman of the shadows? The Spirit was alive within her, moving her to contrition, faith, and love. Jesus had touched her soul before she ever dreamed of anointing his feet. The Pharisees looked down upon her world with disdain; Jesus looked into it with compassion. They saw her intrusion as an act of bold disrespect; Jesus viewed her arrival as an act of courageous love.

Another such occasion of a woman interrupting the course of events occurred just after Jairus, one of the leaders of the synagogue, begged Jesus to come and heal his daughter who lay at the point of death. As Jesus was on the way to Jairus' home, a large crowd of people pressed in on him. Hidden and anonymous in that crowd was a woman who had suffered from a hemorrhage for twelve years. She dared not approach Jesus in public, because she was considered unclean and was, therefore, not supposed to mix with the people. But the woman was firm in her belief that she would be healed if only she could get near enough to touch Jesus' garment, even if he did not see her! She finally managed to maneuver her way through the crowd and reach out to him, touching the fringe of his garment. "Immediately her hemorrhage stopped; and she felt in her body that she was healed of her disease" (Mk 5:29). Jesus, aware that power had gone forth from him, looked around asking, "Who touched my clothes?"—a puzzling question, given that the people pressed in on him from all sides.

The woman knew then that her presence was no longer hidden. She would be exposed and punished for appearing in public in her condition, but she, like the woman who had anointed Jesus' feet, stood firmly in the midst of the turmoil. Trembling with fear, she told Jesus the whole truth, and he gently said to her, "Daughter, your faith has made you well; go in peace, and be healed of your disease" (Mk 5:34). Her faith had grown in the dark, fertile soil of illness, loneliness, and shame. It was in that experience that she had found her strength. Once again, an unknown woman had unveiled the flame of love and mercy in Jesus.

One of the most unusual scenes in the gospels occurred when Jesus and his disciples were in the district of Tyre and Sidon. As they were walking along, a Canaanite woman from the region came out and started shouting, "Have mercy on me, Lord, Son of David; my daughter is tormented by a demon" (Mt 15:22). What makes this incident unique is that Jesus did not answer her. She continued shouting until the disciples finally asked Jesus to send her away. After all, she was a Canaanite, not one of the Jews. Jesus' response startles us because he said bluntly that he had been sent only to the lost sheep of Israel. He seemed to ignore her. As she insisted more and more, he told her, "It is not fair to take the children's food and throw it to the dogs." Undaunted, she answered, "Yes, Lord, yet even the dogs eat the crumbs that fall from their masters' table"(Mt 15:26-27).

That astonishingly humble reply moved Jesus deeply, for it spoke volumes not only about her faith but about her life. She was obviously used to being treated as the lowest of the low, and from that vulnerable position she had dared to step out of the shadows and cry for help. Perhaps Jesus spoke to her as he did only to demonstrate her strength of character to the men who surrounded him. He healed her daughter because of the woman's great faith, humility, and persistence.

The incidents in the gospels in which women take center stage are like sparkling gems that lead us behind the scenes into the obscurity from which the women emerged. There, in the darkness of the unrecorded stories of their lives, we can feel the oppression which nourished their courageous faith. They must have heard Jesus that day on the mountain when he said,

> Blessed are the poor in spirit,
> for theirs is the kingdom of heaven....
> Blessed are those who mourn,
> for they will be comforted....
> Blessed are the meek,
> for they will inherit the earth....
> Blessed are the pure of heart,
> for they will see God.
> (Mt 5:3-5, 8)

These women truly lived in the shelter of the Most High, and abided in the loving shadow of their God. Yet they knew that the gifts generated within them by the power of the Spirit were not theirs to keep. They stepped forth from that sheltering shadow and spoke from the truth of their hearts. They acted on their faith and trust, in spite of the prevailing prejudice which worked to hold them in their place.

These were women steeped in the word of the Scriptures, formed by the experience of their vulnerability and shaped in the cauldron of a male-dominated society that perceived them as weak. A similar encounter with the vulnerable condition of injustice, illness, or loneliness may break open the hearts of modern women and men and lead them to an intimate encounter with Jesus.

Prayerful reflection on the role of women in scriptural events, in the Old Testament as well as in the gospels, opens the door to a deeper, broader understanding of God's all-inclusive mercy and love. It also confirms our conviction of the equality of women and men among the people of God, the Church. As we move then into the wordless moment of contemplation, embraced by God's presence, we will know in our hearts that the power of the Most High overshadows the world and will continue to generate light in the midst of our darkness.

8

Inside the Parables

Layered Meanings

Jesus told the crowds all these things in parables;
without a parable he told them nothing.
This was to fulfill what had been spoken
through the prophet:
"I will open my mouth to speak in parables;
I will proclaim what has been hidden
from the foundation of the world."
Matthew 13:34–35

I have a painting hanging on the wall which depicts a countryside blanketed with red poppies. A road wanders through the valley, past a small, white cottage, into the green, tree-covered hills that ascend into the blue sky. That scene captivates me for a reason I cannot name. It draws me into it so that I almost sense the cool, spring air and feel the texture of the flower petals.

Each person who sees that painting, however, comments on a different aspect of it. Some become very analytical and wonder what kind of flowers cover the fields, which country it might depict, judging from the architecture of the cottage. Others see the road as a symbol of life's journey and speculate on where it may lead. Then there are those who simply savor the peacefulness of the scene without focusing on the details. And, of course, some always ask about the style of painting.

Any form of art speaks many languages and can be heard in the tongue of the audience. Music, dance, art, poetry, and story hold an unlimited potential to touch each person individually. It strikes me that this is one of the reasons Jesus spoke in parables; a less creative and imaginative form of teaching would not have begun to communicate his full message to each listener. Had he attempted to describe the kingdom of heaven, God's mercy and love, and the totality of response required of his listeners, in a prosaic sermon, it would not have been heard, much less felt or remembered. Jesus wanted to touch the heart, not only the mind, of the people, to capture both their attention and their love.

One might say that a parable, like any art form, must be swallowed whole, absorbed by our whole being. It cannot be grasped piece by piece, for it engages the entire person and refers to the totality of the kingdom. If this were not the case, the comparison of the kingdom of heaven to a mustard seed, a treasure hidden in a field, a fishnet, a pearl of great price, and the yeast mixed with flour to leaven the bread, would seem incongruous. How could all of these diverse similitudes refer to the kingdom? Each image Jesus placed before his listeners enclosed a mystical depth that can never be exhausted. Each enfolded the fullness of the kingdom and drew the people into its center.

The word "parable" comes from the Greek word *paraballein* meaning a comparison or a simple story which illustrates a religious or moral lesson. The word *para* means "beside," and *ballein* means "to throw." Thus the message of a parable comes to light as we consider the comparison of two truths which have been thrown next to each other. For example, we may reflect on the price paid for the pearl of great value as symbolic of the sacrifice we must make for the kingdom of heaven. The merchant sold all that he had to purchase the pearl. (Mt 13:45–46). This leads us to a deeper realization of the totality of the commitment required of us if we are to participate in the life of the kingdom. That reflection, however, takes us only so far, as far as the realization of what we must do. We already know that, and it may seem beyond our strength. The parable is intended, however, to lead us more deeply into "what has been hidden from the foundation of the world," and, in fact, to involve us in the kingdom now.

That hidden mystery is beyond words and can only be communicated by such twists of language as paradox, symbol, and hyperbole, for it transcends human comprehension. The mystery far exceeds our understanding, so we can begin to enter it only by letting go and allowing ourselves to be swept away by grace. The parabolic form helps to shake us loose from our grasping for clear, conceptual meanings and the security of the status quo, because the demands and promises we find in the parable are beyond our imagination. The parable can literally turn our lives upside down if we internalize it. It may even make us want to turn our lives upside down! Yet we so often listen to the narrative, think we have grasped its meaning—for it has been explained to us many times—and then turn away satisfied, not knowing what we have missed.

In our effort to internalize a parable, the starting point is a meditative reading of the narrative which gives the obvious, surface level of meaning. Repeated reading and reflection will lead us to notice details and to catch a glimmer of the underlying message disguised by paradox or metaphor. This is where the story begins to come alive and affect us. We experience the fire burning at its core as it illumines the narrative so that it becomes translucent, revealing a more profound reality and warming our hearts. We may wonder at that inner power of the parable as we feel an emotion stir within us, an emotion we cannot name, but which invites an active response. The parable is no longer only a story with a moral lesson but a manifestation of the fullness of the Spirit of God. Now we can embrace it and know it in a unitive sense. The parable is ours.

This process reminds me of the papers I wrote for a French poetry class. A poem, like any work of art, is an attempt to capture and express the intangible. Yet in order to discover its invisible core, we were asked to write an *explication du texte* which forced us to analyze meter, rhyme, figures of speech, and even the feelings elicited by the sound of words with specific vowels and consonants. This dissection of the poem seemed to destroy its beauty, and I felt it would only be useful to one who wanted to learn the techniques of writing poetry. Still, I found it fascinating, somewhat like looking into a mirror from different angles to discover new reflections. By the time my assignment was finished, I knew the poem so well that I found I was reading it as if I were listening to an old friend. Then the intangible began to seep into me and the words of the poet took on a deeper, inexpressible meaning, communicated heart to heart.

Aware now of the prolific possibilities of praying with parables, let us explore the well-known parable of the sower. Since we do not have the version in the original Aramaic Jesus spoke, we are spared the work of analyzing the sounds of the vowels and consonants. If you have a Bible at hand it will be helpful if you turn to the beginning of the thirteenth chapter of Matthew's gospel and spend some time with the parable yourself before continuing.

Jesus was sitting on the shore of the Sea of Galilee when crowds of people heard he was there and came to listen to him. In order to be able to see them and speak to them, he got into a boat and sat down. Of course, he began telling them parables. What better way to hold their attention and convey a lesson. "Listen!" he said,

> A sower went out to sow.
> And as he sowed, some seeds fell on the path,
> and the birds came and ate them up.
> Other seeds fell on rocky ground,
> where they did not have much soil,
> and they sprang up quickly,
> since they had no depth of soil.
> But when the sun rose, they were scorched;
> and since they had no root, they withered away.
> Other seeds fell among thorns,
> and the thorns grew up and choked them.
> Other seeds fell on good soil and brought forth grain,
> some a hundredfold, some sixty, some thirty.
> Let anyone with ears listen! (Mt 13:3–9)

Beginning with verse eighteen of chapter thirteen, Matthew's text provides one possible meaning for this story. We are told that the seed symbolizes the word of the kingdom. The implications of that straightforward statement are multiple. The word of the kingdom is the Word that emanates from God and, therefore, participates in God's very life. God can only give of himself because he is one and cannot be divided. The sower, then, is God spreading not only words or information about the kingdom, but disseminating himself, grace, and the kingdom, for all are one.

This was no ordinary sower who set out to plant seeds only in the soil that was prepared. This was one who scattered the seeds with exuberant extravagance, so that some fell on the path, others on rocky soil that could not support new life, some in the midst of thorn bushes, and, of course, others on the soil that lay hungry for the seed. There seemed to be no careful selectivity. The farmers in the audience must have wondered at that anomaly. Jesus was, in fact, portraying God himself. The sower and the seed were one and the same. Here we begin to sense the unitive reality Jesus presented.

Do you notice the significance in the detailed description of the types of soil that received the seed? The first was impenetrable, the second was shallow, the third full of the roots of thorn bushes that strangled the tender roots of the seeds, and the fourth was receptive and nourishing. These metaphors clearly reflect the souls of those who receive God's word, yet there is an even more profound intimation in this description of the seed penetrating the soil to varying degrees. As the outer shell of the seed is broken, its roots reach out to absorb the very life found in the soil. Here again we glimpse an inner mystery: we, represented by the soil, as well as the seed, the sower, God, and the kingdom, are united in one life. There is no separation. Yet the degree to which the seed is united to the soil depends on the receptivity of the soil.

With this realization we begin to perceive the integral, unitive light that streams from the center of the parable, encircling it with a radiance that entrances us, drawing us more intensely into its field of energy. We no longer need think only of going to heaven someday in the future, for we are invited to be there now, in the midst of the kingdom, in the midst of God.

One day when the Pharisees asked when the kingdom of God was coming, Jesus replied, "The kingdom of God is not coming with things that can be observed; nor will they say, 'Look, here it is!' or 'There it is!' For, in fact, the kingdom of God is among you" (Lk 17:21). The Greek preposition translated here as "among" is often translated as "within" and presents an even more astonishing reality. We are not only in

God's presence, God is within us! The seed has been sown; our openness determines our participation in the life of the kingdom.

We truly miss the richness and mystery of Sacred Scripture if we read it only as if it means exactly what the words express. It is as if we were to walk by a painting of one of the masters and say, "Oh, there is a picture of a field, or a woman, or a court scene of the middle ages." We would miss the expansive vitality of the work of art waiting to reveal the fullness of the mystery concealed beneath its surface. Only the viewer can release that latent power and realize the depth of reality that lies within the art. Similarly, a musical composition is more than a melody. If we listen to it and allow it to wrap itself around us, we find that it has the power to evoke emotions, to ease tension, or to excite us. A parable, too, can easily be dismissed as only a story with a moral lesson, but if we linger and look more intently into its crevices, we begin to perceive a mysterious sense of oneness. We are held by the invisible magnetism of the all-encompassing love that lies at its core.

Read, for example, the parable of the landowner who hired laborers for his vineyard (Mt 20:1–16). This is the story of the workers who were hired at various times of the day, yet all received an equal wage. We can almost feel the indignation of the workers who labored in the heat of the day and still received no more than those who were hired late in the afternoon. Here again we meet the unitive mystery of the divine. Everyone is invited to participate fully in the kingdom! As we reflect on the parable, we may inadvertently separate ourselves from that reality by focusing only on the qualities of God's generosity, impartiality, and forgiveness in calling all of his creatures into his kingdom. Our challenge is to step inside the parable and allow ourselves to know God's love, to feel the profound reality of participating in divine life.

In modern translations of the Bible such as the New Revised Standard Edition, the Greek word *dēnárion* is translated as "the usual daily wage." However, its literal meaning is "a denarius," a coin commonly used at the time. The symbolism of the landowner giving each worker one circular coin intensifies the unitive impact of the parable. As they each received the one coin, all were enveloped in the mystical kingdom of God, even though they were unaware of the inestimable gift they had been given. Their acceptance of the invitation to work in the vineyard opened the door to unlimited possibilities of sharing in divine life.

With this in mind, as we reread the story we notice the gentleness of the landowner as he invited all whom he met to work in his vineyard. He seemed to have spent the day searching for workers, much as a shepherd searches for his lost sheep. The parable stretches our concept of God to enable us to perceive a God who encompasses, permeates, and unites all of her creatures with a mother's love that knows no bounds.

The ending of the parable leaves us with the same enigmatic statement that preceded the story: "So the last shall be first, and the first shall be last" (Mt 20:16). In other words, there is no first and last in the kingdom; all are drawn into the center. This reverses our sense of justice so completely that we are shocked into the realization that God's love does not fit within the limited boundaries of our thinking. First and last merge into oneness. But that is not the whole story. The parable is a vast canvas on which Jesus portrayed the unitive energy of God who draws everyone into full participation in the kingdom, who offers all of us the same incalculable treasure symbolized by the unitive circle of the one denarius. The story reveals an untold divine reality. It presents infinite implications that impact our daily lives.

As we pray with Jesus' parables, we can begin to grasp the very heart of the meaning only when we ponder the stories deeply enough to be subtly drawn beyond reflection into the field of experiential knowing. Jesus spoke in parables in order to proclaim what had been hidden since the foundation of the world, and to invite us into that inexpressible reality of the oneness of all creation in God.

9

Meeting the Dragon

The Challenge of the Call

Another said, "I will follow you, Lord;
but let me first say farewell to those at my home."
Jesus said to him,
"No one who puts a hand to the plow and looks back
is fit for the kingdom of God."
Luke 9:61–62

These unyielding words of Jesus are reminiscent of his response to Nicodemus, to the rich young man, and to all who want to follow him. Although it seems that he leaves no room for human weakness, when this is read in the context of his other teachings, it takes on a different tone.

It is true that Jesus told his disciples that they must take up their cross, leave their family and their land, and be ready to give their entire self to whatever he might ask of them. This theme runs through all of Scripture, and can only be understood in the context of Jesus' other words. In these teachings, as in the parables and analogies he used to support his message, he often used hyperbole to emphasize his point. This was a common practice of his time. Yet we must be careful to distinguish between his literal and figurative statements.

When we apply Jesus' insistence on an uncompromising gift of oneself to following him, we must keep in mind two things. First, he was speaking to an individual person or group of persons at the time, and second, his words applied not only to the externals of one's life but, perhaps most importantly, to its inner, spiritual focus. For example, when Jesus told the rich young man to go, sell all that he had, give to the poor, and follow him, he knew that wealth was the obstacle that was preventing the man from dedicating himself to spiritual transformation. As we read the passage, rather than thinking, "Oh, that can't apply to me, I have a family to support," it might be better to ponder how Jesus would respond to us. What are the obstacles that are keeping us from deepening our spiritual life, from experiencing a more intimate awareness of our union with Jesus? We may find that it is not the externals of our lifestyle which must be changed first, but rather our inner attitudes and weakness: fear of a total commitment, procrastination, concern about others' opinions, or immersion in work that captivates our attention. These qualities are obstacles that can be more difficult to surmount than the change that was asked of the rich young man!

If we listen to the words of the Spirit spoken in our heart, in Sacred Scripture, in spiritual writing, or in the signs of the time in which we live, we too will be asked to make a total response of our whole being in living the Christian life. There is no other way to be true to our baptismal commitment, but what does this entail? Our choices and actions must be driven by a wholehearted desire to comply with Jesus' teaching; there is no room for compromise. Yet this can only be done within the limits of our individual strength and the graces offered to us. Our true desire to respond to the best of our ability is the root from which transformation takes shape. Hence, we must be careful not to measure our love of God by our actions alone but by the desire which drives our choices.

There is an unwritten law in human life that appears in archetypal images throughout mythology, fairy tales, and all of history: if we want to live fully we must give fully. That is not as terrible as it may seem, for in the words of Francis of Assisi, "It is in giving that we receive." We have been promised true joy and the blessings of eternal life. Why then do we hesitate and want to take our hand from the plow and look back? Because when we live by faith, we must make the path while walking. It is frightening to risk walking into an unknown future, even though we believe that we are being led by a loving God. I remember that as I left my professional work and was about to move into a hermitage to live a contemplative life, I said to a friend, "What if I get there and can't pray?" It was a moment of panic before beginning the lifestyle I had dreamed of for so long! My friend only laughed at the idea, and quickly brought me back to reality.

Some who have had the courage to follow God's call, to walk an unfamiliar path, and to encounter hardship along the way without turning back are considered very ordinary people, while others are thought of as saints, heroes, or people of extraordinary wisdom. These are the ones we are aware of because from earliest times their stories have been told, sometimes cloaked in the symbols of mythology and fairytales, as well as in the tomes of history. Scriptural narratives are no exception. In many of these diverse writings, the archetypal image of the hero meeting the dragon serves as a familiar motif, even as it depicts moments in our own lives.

We, as Christians, are called to embark on our own hero's journey which lasts a lifetime, and face our personal dragons which threaten to turn us away from our destination. Then there are mini-journeys which may last for a day, a month, or for years, and which lead us to a new threshold in our personal development where vistas of opportunity stretch before us. There may be a time during which we need to accept pain and illness, struggle through fatigue, or dispel inexplicable anxiety. We are faced with the dragons of mood changes, anger, and greed. Each challenge that presents itself tempts us to turn back through avoidance, denial, or the simple distractions of a movie or a good novel that takes us temporarily out of our reality.

These tests of our courage are but segments of the principal journey that comprises our entire life. Each test helps us develop the strength and integrity required to be faithful to our primary call, no matter what difficulty we face. While the journey takes on a unique shape for each individual, it is always a call to live out our baptismal charism in fidelity to our God. With our acceptance of that call, we are given the wisdom and the courage to follow our path in life with all of its turnings and to continue until the promise of our resurrection into eternal life is fulfilled as we return home bearing the mark of heroes.

Because the hero's journey is an archetypal motif that threads its way through everyone's life, it is also present in Scripture in the stories of ordinary people who were faithful to their call in an extraordinary way, as well as in the stories of their struggles, doubts, and failure. All of these glimpses into the lives of others serve as reminders of our own way of meeting and responding to experience, and offer encouragement as we read of the faithfulness of our God.

The basic pattern of the journey has three stages and begins with a call to set forth. Within our life journey, this might translate into a need to let go of an attachment that impedes our progress, into an invitation to assume an unfamiliar lifestyle that fills us with paradoxical desire and dread, or into a conviction that we must work to correct an injustice that burdens many. Our challenge is not unlike the call of the prophets to speak out against wrong, the call of Mary to walk bravely into an unknown future, the call of the fishermen to leave their boats and to follow Jesus.

Once the journey has begun, we find ourselves in the second stage on the path of trials, and we come face to face with the dragon that we must overcome if we are to continue. In *Mysterium Coniunctionis*, Carl Jung warns us that "In myths the hero is the one who conquers the dragon, not the one who is devoured by it. And yet both have to deal with the same dragon. Also, he is no hero who never met the dragon or who, if he once saw it, declared afterwards that he saw nothing." If we turn away or try to avoid the difficulty that blocks our way, we will only face it again in our life. Escaping from a dragon does not slay it!

The journey ends with the third stage, the return home, which may present its own difficulties. The hero is no longer the same person she was when she answered the call. Confrontation with our dragons leaves its mark upon us. One who has walked the path of trials has also received the gift of a central transformation, expressed perhaps in her compassion, patience, understanding, and wisdom. Those who knew her may not know how to accept these qualities in her, and may turn away in their uncertainty. This is ironic! One would expect to be praised and welcomed, but change in a person is often misjudged. One who has taken a step forward on the path of transformation is sometimes perceived as a threat because he or she is a reminder to others of what they have not done. Of course, they often cannot name this discomfort, but it nags them on the unconscious level.

John the Baptist, who was acclaimed as a prophet, was eventually beheaded. The apostles, who received the Holy Spirit at Pentecost, began to preach the word and to heal, yet they were persecuted. Jesus was crucified because his truth was upsetting the status quo. We may meet a similar reaction, although it will take a far different form and perhaps go unnoticed by the world in general.

Thus while the final stage of the life-journey or the mini-journey is a resurrection from the death to self that one has experienced, the hero is not always recognized, believed, or accepted because he or she still appears to be very ordinary. The hero certainly does not feel like a hero. The transformation that has taken place is hidden deep within one's heart, known to the individual only as a peaceful conviction that she has responded to the invitation of the Spirit to step into a new stage of her life.

The symbolic depiction of the journey that everyone undertakes in life is true at both the psychological and the spiritual level. Whether one speaks of the individuation of the person or of the stages of spiritual development, the same paradigm holds true. For that reason, the stories of the human and spiritual struggles recounted in Scripture serve as a priceless mirror in which we can come to know ourselves and recognize our own dragons.

It is helpful to consider our whole life as a path that leads to eternal life, and to reflect on how we have accepted challenges in the past. Remembering our tenacity as well as our hesitancy gives us confidence to continue the journey with a deeper trust that God never tests us beyond our strength. It is sometimes easier, however, to focus on one part of the journey at a time, viewing it within the larger framework of our life. The basic pattern of three phases will still hold true. There is always the call, which may present itself as realization of a task to be undertaken, a fault to be overcome, or a commitment to be made. Then there is the path of trials on which we encounter the resistance within us and struggle to be faithful to our call by naming and confronting the challenge. The last part of the journey, referred to as the return home, can be an interior integration, a resolution of tensions and conflicting forces.

We will consider here and in the next chapter some examples from Scripture which will illustrate these phases. Before you continue reading, reflect for a moment on an incident or a parable in Scripture which has always intrigued you, or on any passage that first comes to mind. This may be a mirror into which you need to look more deeply. Almost any incident that strikes you will relate to some part of your own hero's journey. Your very attraction to it indicates that it is touching some quality, memory, fear, or desire within you.

For example, one that often haunts me is the story of the rich young man who came to Jesus and asked, "Good Teacher, what must I do to inherit eternal life?" Jesus told him that he must keep the commandments, but the man replied that he had kept all of them since his youth. Then Jesus, seeing his readiness, called him to set out on the hero's journey. "You lack one thing; go, sell what you own, and give the money to the poor, and you will have treasure in heaven; then come, follow me" (Mk 10:17–31). All we are told is that the man became sad because he was very rich. Does that story linger in my mind because I, like the rich young man, am unwilling to make a total commitment? What am I holding back? All that I own includes much more than material possessions. It involves my lifestyle, my ministry, others' respect for me, and certainly the attachment to my own routine and comfort. It probably includes other attachments which have become so habitual that I am not even aware of them. Some aspect of that incident touches a deep part of me which I prefer to ignore and yet long to release, the dragon that blocks my way to more intimate union with God.

When one answers a call and puts a hand to the plow, looking back or hesitating only leads to unhappiness and restlessness. No matter how one tries to ignore the call, the truth of what one has heard lingers in the heart, never to be forgotten. There are many examples of such hesitation in Scripture, and that is encouraging, for we read that people are given another chance, another grace, another call. For example, Peter faced fear when Jesus was arrested and he denied that he knew him, but later he acknowledged his failing.

Then, too, we read of Moses whose curiosity led him to approach the fire in the wilderness. He saw a bush that was burning without being consumed, and he thought, "I must turn aside and look at this great sight, and see why the bush is not burned up." When God saw that Moses had taken the first step by approaching the fire, God called to him from the midst of the flames. Moses bravely responded, "Here I am." That expression of his readiness to listen led God to tell Moses who was speaking to him and explain why God had called his name. God had a mission for Moses, one that Moses did not want to accept. He tried every excuse possible, but, of course, God had an answer for each one. Finally Moses agreed to undertake the journey back to Egypt where he would face the Pharaoh and lead his people out of captivity. On that journey he confronted his own weakness and grew to depend more and more trustingly on his God (Ex 3:1—4:2).

God's word is a blazing fire that burns and purifies but does not consume us. If we dare to approach it, whether out of curiosity or out of a desire to be warmed and comforted by its flame, we will hear God's voice. At times it will startle us, challenge us, make us want to turn away, while at other times it will strengthen and encourage us gently with its eternal beauty and truth. But it will always cause our hearts to burn within us. We too will be set on fire, but never consumed. In that fire we will hear a call to be faithful to our commitment or to set out on a new segment of our journey.

To read Sacred Scripture is to hold a handful of fire. Like Moses we will find that it does not destroy, but rather it transforms us. The voice of God that we hear through the flames reveals to us our true name and our true self. Gazing steadfastly into the fire, into the vibrant, translucent flames that are continually transformed into new colors and shapes, we will hear God's call and receive the grace to set out on the journey only we can make. We will not allow ourselves to take our hand from the plow and look back.

10

Journeying
Personal Spiritual Paths

Then I heard the voice of the Lord saying,
"Whom shall I send,
and who will go for us?"
And I said,
"Here I am; send me!"
Isaiah 6:8

I sometimes think that each of us heard this familiar refrain, "Whom shall I send?" before we were born. Each of us eagerly responded, "Here I am; send me!" Then we set off on our journey, forgetting at first why we were here or where we were going. Gradually, as we matured, we began to hear the voice of the Spirit whispering within us, giving us direction, urging us to be about the task that lay before us.

There are so many examples in Scripture of the women and men who answered, "Here I am," and who were faithful to the task set before them. Those who recorded their stories gave us the details of the external events of their journeys, but often did not describe their inner ordeals. The deepest part of the experience of each person in Scripture lies hidden on the page, just as our own feelings are concealed in our hearts. Reading the stories of the women and men of biblical times, we must listen closely to hear the unexpressed fear, uncertainty, and reluctance, as well as the conviction, courage, commitment, and excitement that underlie their journeys. Then we will be able to see ourselves reflected in the mirror of the narrative, and receive direction and inspiration for our lives.

It is important to remember that the emotions that swirl in our hearts can be either obstacles or stepping-stones, depending upon our perspective. Praying with the scriptural stories can help us observe our own choices and behavior from a new vantage point. It remains for us to hear the resonance that brings them to life by spending time with the text rather than skimming over the surface.

For example, we know nothing of the childhood of Mary which prepared her to accept the monumental task of being the virgin mother of Jesus. Yet the many portrayals we see of Mary at the moment of the angel Gabriel's visit can lead us to picture her arrayed in a beautiful gown, peacefully kneeling at her prie-dieu, absorbed in prayer. I once gave a talk on Mary in which I attempted to bring her down from the pedestal on which we have placed her and portray her as an ordinary woman of her time. After the presentation, a woman came up and thanked me, saying that she had never before thought of Mary as a real Jewish woman. If we lose the realization that even the saints and heroes of biblical times were real human beings, just as we are, we will not see their lives as models for our own.

The story of Jesus also offers only a hint of his early childhood, and then resumes when he is about thirty years old, focusing on his public ministry, death, and resurrection. We are left to wonder about his "hidden life." Then, his apparent reluctance to respond to his mother's comment that the wine had run out at the wedding feast in Cana, gives us cause to read between the lines. We wonder whether he sensed that this was his call to work his first public miracle and to set off on the path that would lead to his crucifixion. It is also true that while reading the gospels we tend to focus more on Jesus' miracles and preaching than on the nights spent in prayer, or on the risk he took in confronting the Pharisees and criticizing their interpretation of the Jewish law. He was human as well as divine, and he experienced the ridicule of many as well as the adulation of his followers.

When the words left unsaid are imagined and felt in our hearts, the people who seem to move effortlessly through sacred history like characters in a play begin to take on flesh and bone; we can perceive their joys and sufferings, fidelity and failings. Their lives then relate more poignantly to our own journey.

Because the Bible is a literary work as well as the inspired word of God and a history of a people, the written accounts of significant figures—especially those of Old Testament times, such as Sarah, Jacob, Deborah, and Solomon—recall some of the literary devices of the great epics like the *Iliad*, the *Odyssey*, and the *Song of Roland*. The heroic qualities are emphasized and the less admirable or simply human qualities, while not being denied, fade into the background. Bringing these qualities into balance as we pray with Scripture makes the stories more realistic. The people of Scripture were real people who were often tired or hungry, discouraged and worried about the future, just as we sometimes are.

Unfortunately, we are given only fragments of women's stories in the Bible, and even those glimpses into their lives are seen through the lens of the patriarchal culture in which they lived. A woman's worth was measured by her ability to bear children; those who could not have children lived in disgrace. Those women whose accomplishments are described in detail were most often the ones who proved they had the cunning and strength of a man, for example Judith and Esther. Even Rebekah is best remembered for telling her son Jacob to deceive his father so that he, instead of his brother Esau, would receive his father's inheritance.

For these reasons, we must be especially careful to read between the lines when we search for women heroines in Scripture. There are many holy women who were faithful to their God and who exerted a major influence on the men whose stories we know so well. Imagine the courage of Moses' mother, who risked her own life to save the life of her son when Pharaoh ordered all male children of the Hebrews to be killed. The lives of such women are forgotten because they are obscured by the values and perspectives of a unique time in history.

Today as women still struggle to be recognized as equal to men, we forget the progress women have made through the centuries in that regard. In Rachel's time, for example, women's lives were separated from those of the men, except when they served them or when a man chose to call for a woman. They lived in separate tents, did the work expected of a woman, and normally had no say in the decisions of the group. This is graphically described in Anita Diamant's novel *The Red Tent*, in which she chronicles the lives of the wives of Jacob. This situation, of course, had changed by the time in which Jesus lived, but realizing the ongoing difference of cultural values helps one to understand the biblical portrayal of women.

As a model of the spiritual journey through life, the most relevant story for all Christians will always be the life of Jesus. However, one way to refresh our reading of the gospel is to consider the life of Joseph, the son of Jacob, because Joseph prefigured Jesus in the Old Testament times. The significant events of his story remind us of the pattern of Jesus' life. It is related in detail at the end of the book of Genesis, chapters thirty-seven to fifty, and reads like a novella. Here I can relate only the highlights of the story.

Among the twelve sons of Jacob, Joseph was always his favorite because Joseph was the firstborn of his beloved wife, Rachel, who had been barren for many years. This, of course, did not make Joseph popular among his brothers. When he naively told them two of his dreams which clearly foretold his future dominance over them, they became even more jealous and decided to take the first opportunity to get rid of him. Jacob inadvertently contributed to their plan one day when he decided to send Joseph to his brothers who were at Shechem pasturing the flock. He called Joseph who responded with the archetypal statement of the biblical hero, "Here I am." Jacob said to him, "Go now, see if it is well with your brothers and with the flock; and bring word back to me"(Gn 37:13–14). So Joseph set off on a journey which was to last a lifetime and, in the end, would make it possible for him to save his own people.

When his brothers saw him in the distance, they said to one another, "Here comes this dreamer. Come now, let us kill him and throw him into one of the pits; then we shall say that a wild animal has devoured him, and we shall see what will become of his dreams" (Gn 37:19–20). After they had carried out their plan, however, they saw a caravan of Ishmaelites on their way to Egypt. They decided to sell Joseph to them for twenty pieces of silver, so they would not be guilty of killing their own brother.

Joseph was later sold to an official of Pharaoh, falsely accused of attempted rape by the official's wife, and thrown into prison. There, it was once again his ability to interpret dreams which brought about an abrupt change in his life. When Pharaoh sought an explanation of two of his own dreams, the Hebrew slave's wisdom was brought to his attention. Joseph listened to the dreams and warned Pharaoh that they foretold seven years of plenty followed by seven years of famine. He recommended that the Pharaoh select a wise, discerning man and set him over all of Egypt to prepare for the famine. Pharaoh said to his servants, "Can we find anyone else like this—one in whom is the spirit of God?" So he made Joseph second only to himself, and set him in command over all of Egypt. Joseph was thirty years old as he began this work. When the years of famine arrived, Pharaoh said to all the Egyptians, "Go to Joseph; what he says to you, do" (Gn 41:1–57).

In the beginning of this story we are reminded of another Joseph, the father of Jesus, who because of a dream took Mary and Jesus into Egypt, a place of exile from which Jesus would emerge to save his people. But the figure of the favorite son of Jacob soon evokes the figure of Jesus himself, the beloved son of his heavenly Father, who is also sent to tend to the welfare of his Father's flock. He, too, is then betrayed and sold for thirty pieces of silver.

The parallels ripple throughout the story of Joseph who, like Jesus, began the central part of his journey at the age of thirty. Even the words of Pharaoh to the people, "what he says to you, do," are echoed in the words of Mary which opened the way for Jesus to provide wine for those who had run out of supplies. As the story continues, Joseph's brothers are sent into Egypt to buy food, for the Hebrews are also suffering from the famine. Once there, however, they do not recognize their brother, who provides them with all that they need. So also, Jesus was not recognized as the son of his Father.

When Joseph was thrown into a pit by his brothers, and then sold as a slave and taken into Egypt, he had died to his former life. Later he was able to "rise again" and save his people, even though his brothers did not recognize him when they went to beg for food. This resonates strongly with the life of Jesus who "emptied himself, taking the form of a slave" (Phil 2:7). He, too, had been taken into Egypt and later suffered death, was placed in a tomb, and rose again that he might save his people from death.

Joseph's story clearly foreshadows the life of the Messiah, and gives us new insights into the gospel narrative. Reflecting on it from this perspective, we cannot help but see that even our own lives were foreshadowed in the actions of those who interacted with Joseph. We, like his brothers, can be jealous of others; we can fail to recognize Jesus in our lives; we turn to him only when we are in need. In much the same way, we see ourselves mirrored in the people of the gospel story. Although at times we may be like those who betrayed Jesus, we also go to him to show us the meaning of our lives, our dreams, and we depend on him for our spiritual and material sustenance. Our actions may be reflected in the doubting Thomas, in the repentant Magdalene, or in the response of the apostles at Pentecost who said in their hearts, "Here I am, send me." We see ourselves in Mary, as we encourage others' faith in Jesus by saying, "Do whatever he tells you" (Jn 2:5).

Scriptural stories, whether accounts of an individual experience or parables, are wellsprings of insight that can refresh us as we thirst for a deeper prayer and union with God. If we approach the life-giving water with faith and pray, "Here I am, Lord," the solid, rock-like surface of the story will split open again and again before us, releasing the spiritual refreshment for which we long. Then we will be strengthened to continue our journey.

These wellsprings of grace that flow from a prayerful reading of Scripture will sometimes move us into the silence of contemplation where we will experience the transforming ardor of the fire of the Holy Spirit. Resting there we will know that we have encountered the divinity that illumines our being. It is that wordless knowing which will affect our relationship to God, to others, and to all of God's creation.

11

Healing with Fire

Divine Energies

He sent out his word and healed them,
and delivered them from destruction.
Psalm 107:20

For neither herb nor poultice
cured them,
but it was your word, O Lord,
that heals all people.
Wisdom 16:12

The word of God is all-pervasive, the very manifestation of the presence of God. It embodies the divine power that creates, transforms, heals, energizes, and infuses all of creation with an incomprehensible participation in the triune divinity. It is filled with the fire to which Jesus referred when he said, "I came to bring fire to the earth, and how I wish it were already kindled!" (Lk 12:49). Yet how lightly we hold it!

Focusing on the healing power of the word, we notice that in Scripture, as in modern times, healing refers to a broad spectrum of ways for restoring wholeness to a person, to a nation, or to the earth. It may refer to the healing of relationships; to the forgiveness of sin; to emotional, psychological, or spiritual healing; as well as to physical healing. In the gospels we read the accounts of Jesus' healing of the paralytic, the man born blind, the woman with a hemorrhage, the lepers, and many who were sick with various diseases, as well as of those cleansed of demons and those raised from the dead. Their inner healing is often only implied, except when Jesus explicitly says, "Your faith has made you whole," or when he also forgives their sins. Yet it is difficult to imagine that there was not a spiritual healing effected by Jesus' compassionate word.

Many who were healed, however, remain almost completely cloaked in the anonymity of their infirmities. Then we hear of Lazarus, Jesus' friend, who died and lay in the tomb for four days before Jesus arrived at the place of his burial. After speaking with Lazarus' sisters, Mary and Martha, Jesus ordered that the stone sealing the entry to the tomb be rolled away, and called Lazarus by name to come forth into the light (Jn 11:43). With a word spoken in the Spirit that filled him, Jesus breathed life into his friend.

That was no ordinary event in the life of Jesus. John created a jewel-like setting for this episode in Jesus' ministry, devoting a whole chapter of his gospel to the sequence of events that surrounded it. Only a reflective reading of the eleventh chapter can lead us inward to experience the symbolism and implications of the moment when Lazarus walked out of the tomb. The raising of Lazarus was a prototype not only of Jesus' death, burial, and resurrection, but of our own. It represented the culmination of all the healing events in the gospels, for in Lazarus, as in Jesus himself, we are shown the ultimate healing that awaits us all, the moment when we too will be renewed and brought forth into the fullness of life that lies deep within us even now.

Healing reaches into the very essence of who we are, for when we are truly healed, we are called by name and made whole again. Any form of healing affects our entire person to some degree. It is a baptismal moment in which we are brought forth from the darkness—whether physical, emotional, or spiritual—into the light of a new day. We are blessed and made holy, for the Word in which we were created has once again renewed our life. In the writings of the Hebrew Scriptures, as well as in the New Testament, a healing often effects a metanoia, or a conversion of one's life. It involves and impacts the whole person, just as an infirmity of any kind touches and changes our life.

The words healed, whole, and holy are all derived from the same

Indo-European root, meaning whole or uninjured. From this root arose several Germanic and Old English words whose meaning centers around that origin, words such as consecrated and blessed. One who is healed has been restored to order and made whole again. The healings recounted in all of Scripture are blessings, because persons wounded in body, mind, or spirit are touched by the Holy Spirit. Whether one's skin is cleansed of leprosy, one's vision or hearing is restored, or one is returned to life, this may be only the first phase of a process that will lead to a more profound healing or metanoia in which one is consecrated to the path of holiness.

The story of Naaman (2 Kgs 5:1–27), recounted on pages 74–75, is one of the clearest examples in Scripture of the most profound form of healing. It began with the cleansing of Naaman's skin from the lesions of leprosy and ended with the opening of his heart to faith. Naaman, the powerful commander of a great army, became humbled. Stripping himself of his garments of authority, he set aside his aura of superiority and power, becoming everyman. Only then could he bring himself to descend repeatedly into the murky water, thus effecting a profound purification. As soon as he fully complied with Elisha's directive he was healed, "his flesh was restored like the flesh of a young boy, and he was clean." His cleansing affected his spirit as well as his body, for he then stood before Elisha and said, "Now I know that there is no God in all the earth except in Israel." In leaving, he asked to take home two mule-loads of earth that he might offer sacrifice only to the God of Israel (2 Kings 5:8–17).

How often we have prayed for our own physical healing, or for that of a loved one, for the healing of hatred and the ravages of war, of the desperation of refugees. Yet we have often forgotten that the pulsating energies of the healing word spring from the divine Word of God who permeates all of creation. Just as a cut on our finger heals first from within, so also any return to wholeness comes from the depth of our being.

The scriptural stories of those who were made whole again, both physically and spiritually, are charged with an invisible, almost tangible energy that awaits us as we read. We connect with that energy partly because the stories are our own stories. We, too, have been paralyzed by fear, dread, or depression, blinded by pride and desire for success, covered with the leprosy of shame or abandonment. We may even have been held in the grip of a life-threatening illness, or faced with the diagnosis of a progressive disease. We know what it means to plead for strength and wholeness. While the focus of our prayer is usually on hope for a cure by medical intervention or a miracle, that is, an outside source, the example of Naaman reminds us that we must participate in our own healing. In other words, our actions must conform with our prayer. Then, whether we receive a literal response to our prayer, the transformation of our perception of our wound, or a richer understanding and acceptance of the meaning of our suffering, we are healed.

The healing energies of the Spirit pervade those stories, the psalms, the words of the prophets and evangelists, every word of Sacred Scripture. When we pray attentively with those words, as in the practice of lectio divina, allowing them to move our heart, we receive the fire of the Holy Spirit that enkindles our heart with light and hope. Jesus came to heal not only the individual infirmities of the people of his time, but the human condition, a condition we share. He has called us by name, and by his word we are renewed.

In the early chapters of Luke's gospel, the evangelist set the scene for the miracles that Jesus was to perform by emphasizing the divine power that filled him. He tells us that when John the Baptist was preaching and the people asked him if he was the Messiah, he responded, "I baptize you with water; but one who is more powerful than I is coming; I am not worthy to untie the thong of his sandals. He will baptize you with the Holy Spirit and fire" (Lk 3:16). Later, after Jesus himself had been baptized, "the Holy Spirit descended upon him in bodily form like a dove" (Lk 3:22). Then, Jesus was led by the Spirit into the wilderness and, after forty days "filled with the power of the Spirit, [he] returned to Galilee" (Lk 4:1–14). Soon after that in the synagogue of Nazareth, he stood up to read from the scroll of Isaiah: "The Spirit of the Lord is upon me, because he has anointed me to bring good news to the poor" (Lk 4:18). As he finished the reading, he sat down and made the astonishing statement, "Today this Scripture has been fulfilled in your hearing" (Lk 4:21). Luke thus highlights the divine energy of the Holy Spirit embodied in Jesus in order to prepare us for his teaching and ministry, to strengthen our faith in the power of the Word of God.

When John the Baptist associates the Holy Spirit with fire, this points, for one thing, to the electrifying effects of baptism in the Spirit, the very current of energy that would be felt by those who touched Jesus or heard his words. Luke expands on this experience of being touched by the energy of God as he describes the people who came to Jesus to be healed of their diseases. He tells us that "all in the crowd were trying to touch him, for power came out from him and healed all of them" (Lk 6:19).

The image of fire helps us feel the inexpressible power of the Spirit that Jesus promised at the Last Supper to send us. That power came upon the apostles in the form of tongues of fire on the day of Pentecost, inflaming them with love and with courage. It dwells now in all who are baptized and share Jesus' life. Fire cleanses, destroys impurities, warms, enlightens, and transforms.

While writing about the electrifying effects of the fire of divine energy, I am reminded of a terrifying experience I had one night when I was living in a small cabin in the midst of a redwood forest. I awoke suddenly and saw through the windows the red-orange glow of fire surrounding my cabin. I lay there transfixed with fear, unable to move. After an eternal few seconds, the darkness of night returned, and I got up to see what had happened. About fifty feet from the cabin an electric transformer had blown and was still showering sparks on the dry leaves of the forest floor. The explosion of electrical energy had lit up the night with an instant of fire. Yet that was only a faint image of the power of the Holy Spirit which fills the Word of God in the person of Jesus, the Word which we consume in the Holy Eucharist, and which we hold in our hands in the sacred words of Scripture.

The potency of this word is manifest in the story of the Roman centurion who begged Jesus to heal his servant who lay at home paralyzed. When Jesus responded, "I will come and cure him," the centurion answered, "Lord, I am not worthy to have you come under my roof; but only speak the word, and my servant will be healed. For I also am a man under authority, with soldiers under me; and I say to one, 'Go,' and he goes, and to another 'Come,' and he comes, and to my slave, 'Do this,' and the slave does it." Jesus was amazed at the man's faith because he had not seen such faith in anyone in Israel, so he said, "Go; let it be done for you according to your faith" (Mt 8:5–13). The healing energy of the Word of God knows no boundaries.

The words and faith of the centurion continue to echo through the centuries as people of all nations pray at Mass, "Lord, I am not worthy to receive you, but only say the word and I shall be healed." With this prayer we express our faith in the power of Jesus, the Word of God, and in his eucharistic presence. When we ask for spiritual healing, it is a healing that cannot be contained but that ripples out to affect our life and the lives of those around us. As we are healed and filled with the Spirit, those we touch in person or in prayer may also experience healing.

When praying with the words of Scripture or receiving the Word in the Eucharist, we are enveloped in the fire of the Holy Spirit, even when we are blind to its presence and our heart seems without feeling. When through grace we awaken to our spiritual blindness, we, like the blind beggar, call out, "Son of David, have mercy on me…let me see again." Our faith can restore our vision, just as the blind man's faith restored his sight. Jesus may say to us, just as he said to him, "your faith has made you well" (Mk 10:46–52).

The words that lie so quietly on the pages of the Bible that we hold in our hands are blazing, dancing flames of divine love. If only we gaze longingly into their profound inner core, we cannot help but be affected by their beauty and warmth. We will not always feel the flames; our hearts will not always burn within us as we pray. We may have to immerse ourselves in the fire of God's words seven times before we perceive the blessing we have received. This blessing gives us the strength to return to our daily challenges as Naaman returned to his country carrying with him a deeper faith and love, a willingness to offer sacrifice to the one true God, and even two mule-loads of dirt on which to offer that sacrifice.

The very healing that gradually leads us toward wholeness, reordering our fragmented self, is at times a hidden, even painful process. Yet, while healing does not always imply the cessation of pain, it always brings with it the power to bless and consecrate our suffering, transforming it into an expression of our love.

> Heal me, O Lord, and I shall be healed;
> save me, and I shall be saved. (Jer 17:14)

> I will restore health to you,
> and your wounds I will heal. (Jer 30:17)

PART THREE

Being
FIRE

The dawning realization of our oneness with God
comes gradually, lest it overwhelm us.
Yet the revelation of that reality
permeates Sacred Scripture.
Through reflection and prayer
we notice the veil that clouds our vision
becoming more transparent,
that we may experience from time to time
an intuitive, direct knowing:
we are one with God,
and in God, with all of creation.
We are fire!

That inner knowing
gives rise to transformative love
that leads us to respond generously
to the grace of God
and fills us with a unitive light.

In that light we compassionately reach out
to Christ in others, spreading the divine flame.
We awaken to the reality that
we live in the midst of
the mystery of our God.

1

The Vanishing Veil

Sharers in Divinity

But Jesus gave a loud cry and breathed his last.
And the veil of the temple
was torn in two
from top to bottom.

Mark 15:37–38, JB

"Lord, that I may see." From the moment that Adam and Eve were expelled from the Garden of Eden until the moment of Jesus' death on the cross, humanity stood with reverent wonder before the veil that concealed the mystery of the divine presence, and cried out in a loud voice, "Teacher, let me see again" (Mk 10:51). Finally at that earth-shattering moment of Jesus' death on the cross, the plea was answered, the veil separating humanity and divinity was torn apart, making it possible for us to see with new eyes and a new inner vision, to see the glory of God shimmering in all of creation. That ability lies latent within us, however, until the cataracts of doubt and incredulity are removed from our eyes by our burning faith. Only then can we see the radiant reality that lies at the heart of existence and experience a unitive relationship with God that was not yet possible in the times of the old covenant.

When the veil of the temple was destroyed as Jesus breathed his last, the door to infinity was thrown open that humanity might share in the divinity of Christ, just as in the incarnation he entered into our humanity. The circle was completed; a moment in time exploded into eternity, removing all distance and creating an eternal now. We can now read the promises of Yahweh in Jeremiah, Isaiah, and the other prophets knowing that they have been accomplished and that we are experiencing their fruits.

> I shall give you a new heart
> and put a new spirit in you;
> I shall remove the heart of stone from your bodies
> and give you a heart of flesh instead....
> You shall be my people and I will be your God.
> I shall rescue you from all your defilement.
> (Ez 36:26–29, JB)

> They will see the glory of Yahweh,
> the splendor of our God....
> Then the eyes of the blind will be opened,
> the ears of the deaf unsealed,
> then the lame will leap like a deer
> and the tongues of the dumb sing for joy.
> (Is 35:2, 5–6, JB)

Before the veil of the temple symbolizing the covenant of Yahweh with his people was torn asunder, the divine manifestations took on a form that inspired an awe-filled fear: the burning bush, clouds, thunder, lightning, the plagues of Egypt, and the water flowing from a rock, to mention only a few. The people were not ready for a more intimate experience of God's presence.

This was made clear when Moses, praying on the mountain, said to Yahweh, "Show me your glory, I pray." Yahweh answered, "See, there is a place by me where you shall stand on the rock; and while my glory passes by I will put you in a cleft of the rock, and I will cover you with my hand until I have passed by; then I will take away my hand, and you shall see my back; but my face shall not be seen" (Ex 33:21–23). Although Moses had been chosen to lead his people from bondage and was able to communicate freely with Yahweh, his participation in the divine life was limited. The time was not yet ripe for God's full manifestation of himself in the divine Word, and the mystifying transformation that would effect.

Yet even a glimpse of the back of Yahweh left its mark on Moses, so that when Moses came down from the mountain after forty days and forty nights, the skin on his face was so radiant that the people were afraid to come near him. Finally Aaron and the other leaders came when he called to them. After he spoke with them, the others came. He told them what Yahweh had said to him on the mountain, but as soon as he had finished speaking, he put a veil over his face. Thereafter, Moses removed the veil only when he went into Yahweh's presence to pray.

It was the death and resurrection of Jesus that forever removed the veil which concealed the manifestation of divine glory. Consequently, after the resurrection the disciples not only saw the glorified Jesus, but spoke with him and shared a meal. Thomas was even urged to put his hand into Jesus' side that he might be convinced of his actual presence there in the room with them. The disciples on the way to Emmaus spoke with Jesus, and recognized him in the breaking of the bread.

In a letter to the Christians in Corinth, Paul referred to the startling transformation of the relationship of humanity to divinity that was effected by the death and resurrection of Jesus. He wrote that the veil which had previously separated them from their God might now be lifted by Christ.

> Since then, we have such a hope,
> we can act with great boldness,
> not like Moses, who put a veil over his face
> to keep the people of Israel
> from gazing at the end of the glory that was being set aside.
> But their minds were hardened.
> Indeed, to this very day,
> when they hear the reading of the old covenant,
> that same veil is still there,
> since only in Christ is it set aside. (2 Cor 3:12–14)

Paul also explained that the new covenant which we have received, in contrast to the covenant of written letters and law, is a covenant of the Spirit who gives life. Having received that Spirit, "all of us, with unveiled faces, seeing the glory of the Lord as though reflected in a mirror, are being transformed into the same image" (2 Cor 3:18). The astonishing truth of this reality is beyond our understanding but within reach of our faith, if we allow it to rest in our hearts and permeate our very being.

As sharers in the divinity of Christ, we are gradually being transformed into his image unless we intentionally turn away. Paul adds, "It is the God who said, 'Let light shine out of darkness,' who has shone in our hearts to give the light of the knowledge of the glory of God in the face of Jesus Christ" (2 Cor 4:6). Imagine the enthusiasm with which Paul wrote those words. We are permeated by that light. A vibrant faith and an acute awareness of that reality can open us to a renewed vision of our daily life. Then, as our union with Christ intensifies, we become progressively transparent, and that divine light radiates through us to touch everyone with whom we come in contact.

When I was in the fifth grade, it was the custom that all of us who arrived at school before eight o'clock in the morning would attend Mass together. Because the prayers of the Mass were still in Latin at that time and totally incomprehensible to us, we would read the prayers aloud together in English, except during October and May, when we would pray the rosary during Mass. Even at that young age, I always found it difficult to pray so many words so quickly, especially during the celebration of Mass. It was as if there were no time to realize what I was saying. However, I soon discovered an escape. I would attend 7:30 Mass by myself, and then go to the classroom. As the others started off for Mass, I would announce to Sister that I had already been to Mass, and she would allow me to stay behind in the classroom.

As much as I resisted the recitation of the prayers of the Mass aloud with the others, some of the prayers made a lasting impression on me, perhaps because I did not understand them. I remember puzzling over the last gospel, "In the beginning was the Word, and the Word was with God, and the Word was God." That made no sense to me. I also wondered why "In the beginning" was not said at the beginning of the Mass.

But the words that always intrigued me the most were, as I remember them, "that we may become partakers of his divinity as he became partaker of our humanity." Even today when I hear the celebrant pray, "By the mystery of this water and wine may we come to share in the divinity of Christ, who humbled himself to share in our humanity," I am astonished at the audacity of our prayer. The veil has been removed, but there are times when it seems we would be more comfortable if it were still in place. The implications and consequences of living that reality cannot be imagined. We inherited the healthy fear and reverence of God's magnificence; it is innate in our humanness.

Then, I remember Jesus' words to the disciples at the Last Supper:

I have said these things to you
while I am still with you.
But the Advocate, the Holy Spirit,
whom the Father will send in my name,
will teach you everything,
and remind you of all
that I have said to you. (Jn 14:25–26)

I am reassured that although I am not ready to realize the full import of the words of the Mass, the Spirit within me will gradually teach me everything and open me to the experience of sharing in the divine life.

Clues that help us find our way to the center of that mystery are sprinkled throughout the words of Sacred Scripture. If we are to discover them among the familiar texts, we must read the words attentively and listen until our hearts burn within us as happened with the disciples on the way to Emmaus after Jesus' resurrection. Jesus met them on their way home from Jerusalem. Not recognizing him, the disciples told him of the confusing events of the last three days. Seeing their consternation and honest desire to understand, beginning with Moses and all the prophets, Jesus "interpreted to them the things about himself in all the scriptures." It was their desire that opened their hearts to Jesus' words. They begged him, "Stay with us," and share our meal. He accepted their invitation. It was at the eucharistic moment of the breaking of the bread that "their eyes were opened, and they recognized him; and he vanished from their sight. They said to each other, 'Were not our hearts burning within us while he was talking to us on the road, while he was opening the scriptures to us?'" (Lk 24:13–32). The word of God had been broken open and, when Jesus broke bread with them, their hearts were opened to his presence. The veil was removed from their eyes that they might see.

That moment can be repeated in our own lives each time we break open the sacred words of Scripture. The time spent with the Word of God in our hearts is a eucharistic moment of intimate union with God, an indescribable experience in which we can truly savor a deep realization of that unity, if only we are present to the Word and allow our hearts to be inflamed with that divine presence.

The veil of the covenant between Yahweh and the Israelites has been torn away by Jesus' death and resurrection. At that moment in time, even the centurion cried out, "This is truly the son of God!" Humanity can now share in the divine life. With each breath we take, we breathe in the Spirit who will teach us everything, so that with Paul we can say, "it is no longer I who live, but it is Christ who lives in me" (Gal 2:20).

When we open the pages of Scripture and gently, reverently begin to enter into the words even as they enter into our hearts, we are at home, at home because we are known and loved, and we love in return. The words we read are being spoken to us. Praying with the inspired words of Scripture can be a moment of communion in which we relish the reality of being sharers in the divinity of Christ who humbled himself to share in our humanity. We are filled with the living fire of the Spirit. We are the fire!

2

The Fruitful Vine

Oneness with God

Like the vine I bud forth delights,
and my blossoms become
glorious and abundant fruit.
Sirach 24:17

I am the true vine,
and my Father is the vinegrower....
Abide in me as I abide in you.
Just as the branch cannot bear fruit by itself
unless it abides in the vine,
neither can you
unless you abide in me.
I am the vine,
you are the branches.
John 15:1–5

The revelation of our relationship with our Creator spreads throughout Scripture like a living vine sinking its roots deep into the soil of
human hearts and branching out with ever more abundant fruit. It
reaches maturity with an intense clarity in Jesus' words at the Last
Supper, and continues to blossom with a tone of urgency in John's letters and the writings of Paul. A grasp of the new reality of participation
in divine life is the cornerstone of our faith, hope, and love. Through
a developing sense of a loving God, humanity was led gently into an

ever more profound understanding of the possibility of an intimate union with God, a unitive relationship which would be actualized as an individual was immersed in the life of the Trinity in Baptism.

In the second creation account we read that "the Lord God formed man from the dust of the ground, and breathed into his nostrils the breath of life" (Gn 2:7). So from the beginning when humanity received the very life of God, Adam and Eve were graced with a glimpse of their participation in divine life. Yet when they were banished from the garden where they walked and communed with their Creator, a rift occurred in that relationship. After that, God was perceived most often as one who dwelt far away in the heavens above, one who watched, punished, and protected.

This was an image of a loving God, yet one who was inaccessible and approached only with awe; one who offered shelter in the storms of life, yet one who demanded sacrifice and who had to be appeased. Browse through the books of the Old Testament and notice the references to God such as these:

O, Lord, look down from your holy dwelling. (Bar 2:16)

For your dwelling is the heaven of heavens. (3 Mc 2:15)

The Lord is exalted, he dwells on high. (Is 33:5)

The Lord is in his holy temple. (Ps 11:4)

I will bow down toward your holy temple
in awe of you. (Ps 5:7)

O Lord our God, you answered them;
you were a forgiving God to them,
but an avenger of their wrongdoings. (Ps 99:8)

But, now and then, the veil was parted and the light of wisdom again streamed into the world. Promises made through the prophets planted a seed of hope in the hearts of the Israelites. As we read in the previous chapter Yahweh said to them:

A new heart I will give you,
and a new spirit I will put within you;

and I will remove from your body
the heart of stone
and give you a heart of flesh.
I will put my spirit within you,
and make you follow my statutes
and be careful to observe my ordinances. (Ez 36:26, 27)

With these words God promises not to remain at a distance but to put his Spirit within us. Prophecies like this continue echoing through the ages. Yahweh speaks through prophets in the eternal present so that what was promised to the Israelites at a particular time in history, is spoken to us at this very moment. In God the present and the future are one. Our human linear way of thinking makes it difficult for us to grasp the unity of all time.

Paul seemed to be writing of the fulfillment of this prophecy of Ezekiel in his letter to the Romans, as he strongly emphasized the dwelling of the Spirit within us. He described over and over again the effects of this life of the Spirit, especially in the eighth chapter. "But you are not in the flesh; you are in the Spirit, since the Spirit of God dwells in you" (Rom 8:9). Reflecting on that chapter can help us realize the marvelous implications of this truth.

In his letters Paul repeatedly described the new reality of our relationship with God made possible by the death and resurrection of Jesus, often using images that were familiar to the people. For example, writing to the Corinthians, he picked up the image of the temple and extended it: "Do you not know that you are God's temple and that God's Spirit dwells in you?" (1 Cor 3:16). The people no longer had to look on high for a God who dwelt in the heavens. In his next letter he wrote, "For we are the temple of the living God; as God said, 'I will live in them and walk among them, and I will be their God, and they shall be my people'" (2 Cor 6:16). Here Paul was telling a group of Gentiles of the promise Yahweh repeated in Leviticus 26:11–12 and Ezekiel 37:27. The notion of tender intimacy with God was not entirely absent in the Old Testament, but too often the sense of distance between God and humanity overshadowed it.

Paul was careful to be especially clear when he was writing to the Gentiles who did not share the scriptural heritage of the Jews. For example, he reassured the Ephesians that although they were Gentiles by birth and, therefore, "at that time without Christ, being aliens from the commonwealth of Israel, and strangers to the covenant of promise, having no hope and without God in the world," they were no longer separate. He continued, "But now in Christ Jesus you who once were far off have been brought near by the blood of Christ. For he is our peace; in his flesh he has made both groups into one and has broken down the dividing wall, that is, the hostility between us" (Eph 2:12–14).

Having emphasized that Jews and Gentiles are united in the one body of Christ, he returned to the image of the temple of which Christ is the cornerstone. "In him the whole structure is joined together and grows into a holy temple in the Lord; in whom you also are built together spiritually into a dwelling place for God" (Eph 2:21–22). This temple recalls the symbol of the living vine through which the same life flows through the trunk and the branches. It can be difficult to experience the full implications of these statements we have heard so often. Yet if we pause to let them resonate in our hearts, we can gradually reach a deeper appreciation of the truth Paul was trying to convey.

It is true that in the gospels Jesus speaks of his Father at times as if he were far away, looking down upon his creation. For example, when the disciples ask him to teach them to pray, he says "Pray then in this way: Our Father in heaven, hallowed be your name." Notice, however, that he begins by cautioning them not to "heap up empty phrases as the Gentiles do…for your Father knows what you need before you ask him" (Mt 6:7–9). Here there is an intimation of the unitive reality that Jesus would make so explicit the night before he died. He prepared his listeners gently for the astonishing revelation that was to come: "On that day you will know that I am in my Father, and you in me, and I in you" (Jn 14:20).

This is a transformative reality in which we now share through baptism. When we grasp the astounding ramifications of the sacrament, they shatter our somewhat comfortable, habitual manner of putting God at a distance, calling upon God only when there is a need, praying when it is convenient. One truth that flows from that reality is that if we are one with God, we are one with each other. The division between our neighbor and ourselves dissolves. That realization can change our view, not only of ourselves but of all humanity, for our neighbor shares God's life, our life; the person starving in Africa is part of us; the Tibetan monk prays with us.

This unitive perception of all reality effects a profound change deep within us, making it possible for us to live the fullness of life and to break out of our habit of immersing ourselves only in the events of our own lives. Our horizon is broadened and we can no longer separate ourselves from the suffering, the poor, and the homeless of the world, nor can we ignore the violence being done to the universe. While it is true that a new possibility of full participation in the divine life is opened to us through the sacrament of baptism, it is important to remember that there is another sense in which all of creation shares that life and is united in the ground of divine being.

At the Last Supper Jesus prayed that we might all be one. "As you, Father, are in me and I am in you, may they also be in us, so that the world may believe that you have sent me" (Jn 17:21). The crescendo of this unitive motif rises to a climax as Jesus continues to pray for oneness:

The glory that you have given me I have given them,
so that they may be one, as we are one,
I in them and you in me,
that they may become completely one,
so that the world may know that you have sent me
and have loved them
even as you have loved me. (Jn 17:22–23)

Only through grace can we even begin to grasp the implication of this astounding revelation and allow it to affect our daily lives.

That same evening Jesus searched for an image to imprint upon his disciples' memories the reality that they truly participated in the divine life and thus were also one with each other. Using an image familiar to all of them, he explained, "I am the vine, you are the branches" (Jn 15:5). The same vital energy runs through the whole vine, and what is done to one branch affects every part of the vine.

Indeed we, like the branches dependent on the trunk of the vine, could not live except through our participation in the very life of God who breathed his Spirit into our first parents, the Spirit who "pervades and penetrates all things. For she is a breath of the power of God, and a pure emanation of the glory of the Almighty" (Wis 7:24–25). But perhaps the words, "The glory that you have given me I have given them," best express the new level of our likeness to God which is bestowed upon us at baptism. Humanity was created in God's image, but we now share God's glory!

The reference in the Last Supper discourse to the living vine which bears fruit abundantly is a moving effort on Jesus' part to help his disciples grasp the wondrous, almost unthinkable, reality that they were one with him just as he and the Father are one. He was going to leave them for a while, but they could never be separated from him, for they shared in the same breath of life, in fact, in the glory of God.

It was because of this that he could say to them and to us, "Peace I leave with you; my peace I give to you. I do not give to you as the world gives. Do not let your hearts be troubled, and do not let them be afraid" (Jn 14:27). What greater peace could there be than one that springs from a realization of one's union with God?

Prayerful reflection on this astonishing unitive reality opens the door of our heart to an ever more profound experience of that unity, of the divine life that flows through us. Making that truth part of our lives shatters our complacency and challenges us to a greater awareness of the responsibility that flows from the gift we have received. Let us continually savor that reality so that it might transform us and bear fruit in our lives.

3

An Inner Knowing

Beyond Understanding

I have been crucified with Christ;
and it is no longer I who live,
but it is Christ who lives in me.
And the life I now live in the flesh
I live by faith in the Son of God,
who loved me and gave himself for me.
Galatians 2:19–20

With these words Paul is trying to take us beyond our usual way of knowing into the realm of faith, where we are called to leave behind the safety net of the familiar and allow ourselves to be immersed in a new reality. If we choose to cling to that safety net, which usually serves us well, we will be confined by the limitations of human understanding. We will remain on the surface of the scriptural words, never penetrating into the depth of meaning that Paul intends.

It is not always necessary to fully understand a scriptural passage in order to feel its intensity. In fact, it is not always possible because the deepest meaning of some passages is beyond words, outside the boundaries of our experience. The meaning dwells in the realm of inner knowing which we often do not trust, or which perhaps we do not recognize. That inexplicable knowing is a gift of the Spirit of wisdom who Jesus promised would guide us into all truth (Jn 16:13).

Sometimes we feel that we "get nothing out of" some parts of Scripture because we measure the fruitfulness of our reading by our ability to understand the meaning of the passage. At such times, if we pause and re-read the words phrase by phrase, we may find that we begin to hear a whisper, to feel a movement in our heart. The word of God is affecting us deeply without our being able to name the experience.

For years I found reading the Pauline letters difficult, because their meaning seemed too dense, too obtuse for me to integrate and apply to my daily life. The problem was that I was trying too hard and my own efforts were not enough. Now I find that if I relax and move slowly through the words, holding them and resting in short passages, the Spirit often touches me at a profound level. I experience a connection, a knowing which I cannot describe, but for a moment it pervades my being. It can only be savored.

It was to this kind of knowing that Jesus was referring when he told the apostles at the Last Supper, "you know the way to the place where I am going." Thomas took him literally and responded, "Lord, we do not know where you are going. How can we know the way?" He understood only the human way of knowing, but Jesus, after explaining that he himself was the way, went on to talk about a deeper knowing. "If you know me, you will know my Father also. From now on you do know him and have seen him" (Jn 14:4–7). This astonishing truth can be internalized and embraced only by a mode of knowing that goes far beyond the limitations of human comprehension, for it is more experiential than intellectual. It is felt with the heart rather than grasped by the mind.

For example, when Paul wrote, "I have been crucified with Christ, and it is no longer I who live, but it is Christ who lives in me," he was not describing the effect of a personal mystical experience. He was referring to a reality which is accessible to all of us, although it is beyond even our imagination. Attempting to explain this truth, Paul leads us into even deeper waters:

Do you not know
that all of us who have been baptized into Christ Jesus
were baptized into his death?
Therefore we have been buried with him
by baptism into death,
so that, just as Christ was raised from the dead

> by the glory of the Father,
> so we too might walk in newness of life....
> But if we have died with Christ,
> we believe that we will also live with him. (Rom 6:3–4, 8)

Paul is not describing a future time, for we are living the life of Christ now. Baptism is a unitive moment of both death and resurrection, so we can truly say with Paul that "it is no longer I who live, but it is Christ who lives in me." While it is relatively easy to repeat and even to believe those words, their ramifications will only gradually penetrate our consciousness more and more profoundly as we try to live according to that reality. The grace of baptism has transformed us, has brought us into a new level of being, and has united us with Christ so that we might share his divinity. Grasping that truth, holding it in our heart, and making it a part of our life requires an inner knowing accessible only through faith. We search for certainty and yet sometimes do not recognize it, because some forms of certainty are not founded on logic or science, but on a movement of the heart. We simply know.

Because that knowing cannot be described or explained, others often scoff at it, ridiculing our naiveté. They judge a life lived according to that heart-knowledge as one that is wasted, foolish, or insane. Yet, they admire the kindness, generosity, commitment, and joyfulness of those who live that life, without realizing the source of those qualities: Christ who lives in his followers.

There are countless examples of persons whose lives were manifestations of Christ's life within them, persons as different as Francis of Assisi, Thérèse of Lisieux, Charles de Foucauld, and, in our own time, Mother Teresa of Calcutta. During their lives they were misunderstood and often criticized by others who did not share their awareness of the divine life that gave meaning to their lives. These Christians knew that Christ lived not only in them but in everyone else. That strong conviction shaped their lives, for its implications are endless and astonishing.

Grasping this truth with an inner knowing is like taking hold of a high voltage wire. It causes us to die to ourselves and to say as Christ did, "not my will but yours be done" (Lk 22:42). At the same time, it opens the door to a new life and a new worldview. Nothing is seen as before. Our perception is transformed. On one level, this may not be a comfortable experience, yet on another, it is ecstatic. Francis of Assisi was able to embrace the leper because what before had seemed repulsive was now inviting. He saw Christ in the leper because he had met Christ in himself. His life had become one with the life of Christ. And so he was able to grasp and practice the shattering truth in Christ's words, "Truly I tell you, just as you did it to one of the least of these...you did it to me" (Mt 25:40). Francis could accept these words because his deepest desire was not to imitate Christ but to live Christ's life.

A tremendous power is encapsulated in Paul's simple statement that we have read and heard so often, "it is no longer I who live, but it is Christ who lives in me" (Gal 2:20). Has it penetrated the protective barriers that we have constructed, perhaps unconsciously, to keep ourselves secure and comfortable in our safety net of the familiar? Has it pierced our hearts?

Paul is relentless in proclaiming the fusion of our lives with Christ's life. It is the central theme of his letters, and weaves through his writing as the core of his teaching because it gives meaning to Christian life. In his letter to the Corinthians he tells them that "those who are spiritual discern all things, and they are themselves subject to no one else's scrutiny." The reason he gives for this is that "we have the mind of Christ" (1 Cor 2:15–16). Can that be? Living proof is found in the lives of those who make the choices Christ would make, regardless of the circumstances or of the challenges presented by those choices.

For example, when Mother Teresa made the radical decision to leave the security of her religious community and live among the poor of Calcutta, she was acting according to the mind of Christ. She knew at a level beyond rational explanation that it was what she must do. It was a dangerous and risky decision that bewildered many, but her life is proof that it was an inner knowing that gave her the assurance and the courage to carry it out. This inner knowing is an emanation of union with Christ. It is a unitive knowing.

The very different ways in which Thérèse of Lisieux and Charles de Foucauld lived out their lives in Christ, one in a cloistered community and the other in the solitude of the desert, demonstrate the endless variety of ways in which identification with Christ may evolve in one's life. Thérèse and Charles also made choices dictated by a profound, inexplicable knowing that enabled them to follow their call. Every Christian is called to live the life of Christ; only the circumstances and the form of each one's life vary.

In the first two chapters of Paul's letter to the Colossians, he enlarges upon the theme of our union with Christ, describing it in terms that are almost too overwhelming for us to absorb. This truth can only be internalized and lived out through grace which opens us to the mystery, the mystery which is Christ in us. Paul yearned

> to make the word of God fully known,
> the mystery that has been hidden
> throughout the ages and generations
> but has now been revealed to his saints.
> To them God chose to make known
> how great among the Gentiles
> are the riches of the glory of this mystery,
> which is Christ in you, the hope of glory. (Col 1:25–27)

This mystery is Christ in you! Paul wrote with an urgency and insistence, reiterating the reality of the Christ mystery that has now been revealed, so that those who read his words might "have all the riches of assured understanding and have the knowledge of God's mystery, that is, Christ himself, in whom are hidden all the treasures of wisdom and knowledge" (Col 2:2–3). His words are charged with an intensity that can so easily be lost in the fog of familiarity which dampens their impact. They must be read slowly, each phrase savored, for the truth that they convey is breathtaking, awesome, and sacred.

Supposing we were told for the first time that in Christ "the whole fullness of deity dwells bodily, and you have come to fullness in him, who is the head of every ruler and authority" (Col 2:9–10). How would we react? Imagine that we hear one day that "When Christ who is your life is revealed, then you also will be revealed with him in glory" (Col 3:4). Would that realization change our perception of the events of our life and the lives of those around us?

As we pray with Scripture, we will often find that the reality described seems beyond us. The fleeting thought, "I don't understand this," may give us reason to skip over the text. Yet what we do not understand in Sacred Scripture is often the very heart of the message, not meant to be understood by our mind but experienced by our heart. There is a transforming power in the words of Scripture. If we stay close to its burning fire, and listen openly with our hearts, the word of God will effect an inner knowing in us. So, in Paul's words,

Let the word of Christ dwell in you richly. (Col 3:16)

4

A Deeper Well

The Source of Life

If you knew the gift of God,
and who it is that is saying to you,
"Give me a drink,"
you would have asked him,
and he would have given you
living water.

John 4:10

"If you knew...." Here, seated at Jacob's well in the heat of the day, Jesus is speaking to a woman of Samaria, gently inviting her to enter the realm of unknowing beyond knowing. She, of course, was totally unaware of the earth-shattering significance of the words this Jewish stranger was saying to her. They made no sense! What was living water?

We can only wonder at the remarkable conversation which took place on that very ordinary afternoon. Reading it from our vantage point in time we may think we know what Jesus meant, but do we hear the mysterious meaning beyond understanding? Plumbing the depths of meaning in Jesus' words is somewhat like reaching into an inexhaustible well. As we reflect on the words, we find ourselves without words, and we may be led into a pregnant silence. There we may even be given a taste of the spring of water that gushes up in us to eternal life (Jn 4:14).

Following the conversation between Jesus and the Samaritan woman is like tracing a spiral from its outer edges to its center.

Beginning with a straightforward request for a drink of water, it circles around through Jesus' offer of living water, his comments on her lifestyle, and a discussion of worship, to the woman's reference to the Messiah and Jesus' direct response, "I am he, the one who is speaking to you." Startled at this straightforward answer, she looked at him and knew he was speaking the truth. There was no logical reason to believe him; she simply knew at a very deep level.

The Samaritan woman had already said, "Sir, I see that you are a prophet." Now she saw that he was speaking the truth. She, therefore, quickly ran back to the city and excitedly said to the people, "Come and see a man who told me everything I have ever done!" In each of these instances the word "see" is used metaphorically to express the concept of an inexplicable, unitive knowing. The woman did not want the people simply to see Jesus; she wanted them to know him. In fact, after seeing him and hearing his words, they said, "we know that this is truly the Savior of the world" (Jn 4:5–42).

Throughout John's gospel the concept of seeing is often used in this sense. In the Prologue, for example, he wrote, "No one has ever seen God. It is God the only Son, who is close to the Father's heart, who has made him known" (Jn 1:18). Shortly after that he tells of the time when two of John the Baptist's disciples, Andrew and probably the evangelist himself, followed Jesus and asked him, "Where are you staying?" Jesus answered, "Come and see." During that visit they came to know Jesus as Messiah, and called others to come and see him (Jn 1:35–42).

Later, in the ninth chapter, John describes in great detail the cure of a blind man, in order to highlight Jesus' comments about spiritual blindness or the refusal to see the truth. Jesus came upon a man born blind and healed him by mixing saliva with dirt, spreading the mud on the man's eyes, and telling him to go and wash in the pool of Siloam. The man "went and washed and came back able to see." We know that he not only saw with his eyes, but that he saw in his heart. When the Pharisees later asked him, referring to Jesus, "What do you say about him? It was your eyes he opened," he replied, "He is a prophet." This incident tells us much more than the fact that Jesus healed the vision of a blind man! Reading the chapter, we notice

John's repeated use of the symbol of sight to represent the inner knowing of faith.

The entire account culminates in Jesus' paradoxical statement, "I came into this world for judgment so that those who do not see may see, and those who do see may become blind." This caught the attention of the Pharisees who asked, "Surely we are not blind, are we?" Looking at them Jesus replied firmly, "If you were blind, you would not have sin. But now that you say, 'We see,' your sin remains" (Jn 9:1–41). In other words, those who see the truth and, nevertheless, refuse to acknowledge it, are held responsible for turning away. Jesus must have looked at the Pharisees and thought, "If you only knew...." The blind man and the Samaritan woman both truly saw Jesus and knew him with the vision of their heart.

Theirs was a unitive knowing that is both direct and immediate, that is, not mediated by the presentation of factual information. For example, we know the beauty of a sunset not because we stop to analyze the difference between it and the noonday sunshine, but through a unitive knowledge; that is, we are drawn into an experience of its beauty and filled with awe, wonder, and stillness. Our knowing emanates from the union itself. It creates wonder in us because there is always an element of unknowing, of mystery, in this knowing. We cannot plumb the depths of it, and we cannot explain it because it springs up inside us and is different from factual knowledge.

The distinction between factual and unitive knowledge might be compared to the difference between knowing a symphony by reading the musical score, and knowing it by listening to its music, allowing it to touch your inner core. That is God's way of knowing.

If we are to know Jesus and receive the living water that he offers us, we can do that only by seeing him, but not only through the insight gained by study or by being told who he is. We truly see him by responding to his invitation to "come and see," and then staying with him. We also see Jesus intimately through his words, not necessarily by understanding what he said, but more importantly by remaining with those words and experiencing them. That experience is not a matter of feeling, but of unitive knowing, a movement of the heart. Through the words of Scripture we know Jesus, the Word of God. Human words fail in presenting this truth, for it lies beyond our usual ideas and concepts, and can only be grasped through unitive knowing.

It was no accident that Jesus met the Samaritan woman by Jacob's well, for centuries a source of life-giving water for God's people. Now Jesus had come into the world to be for all those who believed in him a deeper well that reaches into eternity and taps into the divine source of life. He will provide water that will become, in the heart of all those who partake of it, "a spring of living water gushing up to eternal life" (Jn 4:14).

Jesus himself is the well that reaches into infinity. He is the way through whom we receive the living water of the Spirit and come to know the Father. Speaking of Jesus, Paul wrote to the Ephesians that "through him both of us have access in one Spirit to the Father" (Eph 2:18). How many times have we prayed "through Jesus Christ our Lord" without realizing the significance of those words?

The use of water as a symbol of the Spirit and life appears repeatedly in John's gospel. To name a few instances of this, at the beginning of Jesus' public life he provided wine for the guests at the wedding feast at Cana, but not without first telling the servants to fill the six stone jars with water which he transformed into wine (Jn 2:7). This was his first public miracle; at the end of his life wine would become his life-blood. Soon after the wedding, while Jesus was in Jerusalem for the Passover festival, he told Nicodemus, a Pharisee who came to him by night, that "no one can enter the kingdom of God without being born of water and Spirit" (Jn 3:5). Then, of course, while he was in Samaria, a woman came to the well for water, but Jesus offered her living water (Jn 4:14).

Water is a central focus in other incidents in Jesus' ministry, such as the cure of the sick man who had lain by the pool of Beth-zatha for thirty-eight years (Jn 5:2–25). The sick man, along with the others near the pool, believed that the first one to enter the pool when the water was stirred up would be cured. One is reminded here of the creation account where we are told that "the earth was a formless void, there was darkness over the deep, and God's spirit hovered over the water" (Gn 1:2, JB). These and many other such incidents involving water come into fullness as we are told that after Jesus "bowed his head and gave up his spirit…one of the soldiers pierced his side with a spear, and at once blood and water came out" (Jn 19:30, 34). As he had promised, Jesus gave us his spirit as living water that we might never thirst.

One can't help but notice how the symbolic use of water in Jesus' life foreshadows the baptismal and eucharistic sacraments through which we are born of water and the Spirit as we enter into divine life, and are sustained by being united with body and blood of Jesus, the well that gushes forth living water. Even the use of holy water in blessings carries the meaning embedded in all of these incidents and in Jesus' teachings.

"If you only knew…you would have asked him, and he would have given you living water." All of us are invited to share in the abundance made possible by the opening of the divine well. In fact, it is by drinking of the same Spirit that we are drawn into union not only with Jesus, but with all who live in him. In the sixties, we often sang a popular hymn, accompanied by the strumming of guitar, that expressed this unitive reality: "We are one in the Spirit, we are one in the Lord, we are one with each other…." As those words and melody run through my memory, I wonder if the meaning of the lyrics too often remained at the intellectual level. Of course I believed them, understood them, and, yes, I lived them as best I could, but I wonder how deeply I knew the reality which they described.

Although the inner knowing of a mystery cannot be quantified, it can increase into eternity. There is no end to our unitive experience of the infinite; we never arrive at completion! It seems easier at times, however, to know our own unity with Jesus in the Spirit than it is to include others in that circle of oneness. Ironically, the very humanity of our fellow Christians, their strength and weakness, sanctity and sinfulness, wealth and need, can be a barrier in the realization of our unity. We are called to look beyond, beneath, and within their humanity and to be aware of the indwelling of the same Spirit who lives in us and unites us in one body.

As that awareness sharpens, we realize or perhaps know that we do not live in isolation and that ours is a divine responsibility to the world. Our sensitivity to others may gradually become more intense so that we feel others' needs and their suffering. Then we will find it difficult to turn away. Our perceptions may change as we begin to see and to know through the Spirit, so that our lives take on new vitality, new pain, and a new kind of joy, an inner joy born of a love that surpasses understanding.

This will be possible because one ordinary afternoon we began to drink living water from the deeper well, Jesus himself. We now turn to others and say in wonderment, "If you only knew!"

Seeing Jesus in us, they too may come to know him.

5

A New Creation

The Unfolding Mystery

From now on, therefore,
we regard no one from a human point of view;
even though we once knew Christ
from a human point of view,
we know him no longer in that way.
So if anyone is in Christ,
there is a new creation:
everything old has passed away;
see, everything has become new!
2 Corinthians 5:16–17

Late one Good Friday afternoon I was sitting on my balcony over-looking the smooth, deep blue of the Mediterranean, listening to the somber beat of drums in the distance. As the rhythmic sound drew closer, I looked down and saw the Roman centurions with their soldiers marching through the narrow streets of the small Catalonian town. The repetitive beat and the tranquility of the scene cast a meditative spell over me. It seemed the whole village had been woven into a profound awareness of the reality of the crucifixion, which was made so much more present though the reenactment of the drama.

Then, slowly a reddish gold orb began to rise on the horizon, as if emerging from the deep twilight of the sea. I was entranced as the full moon rose, casting a path of golden light across the water. It was a symbol of resurrection, a promise of fullness of life and of transformation.

Often the sight of the full moon takes me back to that experience in Spain, and I marvel at the silent circle of light emerging out of darkness, presenting a continual cycle of death and rebirth, night and day, winter and spring. The psalmist recalls this continuity as he ponders the faithfulness of Yahweh in gratitude. "You have made the moon to mark the seasons; the sun knows its time for setting" (Ps 104:19). The cyclic nature of the moon, in both its nightly reappearance and its waxing and waning, has long intrigued humanity, giving rise in ages past to the cults of moon goddesses and mythological symbols that spring from its influence on creation. Across cultures the birth, death, and resurrection phases of the moon symbolize immortality, eternity, and perpetual renewal.

How fitting, then, that the date of Easter, the celebration of Jesus' resurrection, is set according to the phase of the full moon, for from the moment of the resurrection a new fullness of life in the Holy Spirit became possible for those who believe in Jesus and are baptized. As I watched the full moon rising and spreading a golden ray of light over the water that Good Friday, I was filled with a sense of awe. Jesus' death had become an entrance into eternal life, so that the light of a new creation might begin to sweep over the world.

At the beginning of time when "the earth was a formless void and darkness covered the face of the deep," God said "Let there be light," pouring forth the divine light to cover the earth (Gn 1:2–3). Then came that redeeming moment when the light of Christ shone from the darkness of the tomb, and creation began to realize its potential. Now all those baptized in Christ share in his Spirit! Even as the fire of the Holy Spirit now burns within all Christians, it is gradually making all things new.

The words of Paul to the Corinthians echo the reality of that newness, a reality that can so easily elude us, yet which has the power to transform our vision and our lives. He writes, "From now on, therefore, we regard no one from a human point of view; even though we once knew Christ from a human point of view, we know him no longer in that way" (2 Cor 5:16).

Here Paul is making a bold, sweeping statement. Read it once more. In baptism we have been gifted with the ability to see all things as Christ sees them, yet it is an ability we are not forced to employ. Christians can easily forget that they have been divinized, that in baptism they died with Christ and now live in him. We profess our belief in that truth, but it is so radical that it escapes our grasp. We can only reach out for it again and again that we may live it. Its impact is endlessly astonishing! Jesus' spirit within us gradually opens our eyes that we may see.

If we truly see everyone and everything from the vantage point of our life in Christ, that perception affects our choices, our actions, and our relationships. Full acceptance of our invitation to participate in the new creation can have a profound impact on our vision of all reality, an impact that has the power to touch our innermost being and transform us. Realizing that can simultaneously imbue us with desire and dread, anticipation and fear that both urge us forward and tempt us to pull back from the edge of that unknown future. It is only in the strength of our life in Christ that we are able to step into the radiant new day and open our eyes to see, as if for the first time.

The veil that shades our vision gradually becomes transparent, so that we can see clearly—when we take time to look. Separation dissolves into unity as we begin to grasp the mystery that there is "one body and one spirit...one Lord, one faith, one baptism, one God and Father of all, who is above all and through all and in all" (Eph 4:4–6). As that truth blossoms from the seed of faith into a lived reality, we begin to glimpse the new creation.

When we adopt this new perspective on life that flows from our incorporation into Christ, it sends out ripples, or perhaps shockwaves that will affect our understanding of the interrelatedness of all humanity and of the whole of creation. It will affect all that we see, all that we do, and all that we feel. The consequences of that new perspective will cause our hearts to begin to move in rhythm with the joys and sufferings of other human beings, the springtimes and winters of the earth, the beauty and the pollution of the universe. With our baptism into Jesus' death and resurrection we become one with him, even to the extent of joining with him in renewing creation, a creation that, as it groans with the pangs of giving birth, begins to experience new life (Rom 8:22–23).

As Paul explains, "So if anyone is in Christ, there is a new creation: everything old has passed away; see, everything has become new!" (2 Cor 5:17). This reminds me of the glorious picture Isaiah painted as he cried out in a prophecy:

> The wilderness and the dry land shall be glad,
> the desert shall rejoice and blossom;
> like the crocus it shall blossom abundantly,
> and rejoice with joy and singing....
> They shall see the glory of the Lord,
> the majesty of our God....
> Then the eyes of the blind shall be opened,
> and the ears of the deaf unstopped;
> then the lame shall leap like a deer,
> and the tongue of the speechless sing for joy. (Is 35:1-6)

That whole chapter from Isaiah bursts forth with a vision of the transformation that will be experienced as all of creation is reconciled to God through Christ. It also vibrates with the resurrected life of the baptized who already share in the life of the glorified Christ.

That realization deepens in us as we pray with Scripture, especially if we are alert for the references to our living the divine life. John's gospel and the letters of Paul in particular are bursting with the magnificence of that truth, so beyond our wildest dreams. For example, remember when Jesus said, "Those who eat my flesh and drink my blood have eternal life...(they) abide in me and I in them"? It was too much for some of his disciples to believe, and they turned away (Jn 6:54-56, 66).

We usually assume that it was the prophecy of the Eucharist that some could not accept, but notice that the second part of the statement is no less difficult to believe. Jesus said that we live in him and he in us, and that we have eternal life. When you read the gospels, notice the metaphoric and literal references Jesus made to our union with him, and spend time with Paul's letter to the Romans, especially chapters 6–8, and with his second letter to the Corinthians. There his message is clear and conveyed with an intensity that reaffirms our belief.

As we rest in the splendorous vision of the magnificent life we share, we are caught up in awe of the indescribable reality of our intimate bonds with all of creation. We move into a deeper awareness of God's presence, while, at the same time, we are drawn into the after-shocks that follow in the wake of our awareness. We are challenged to look around us with the vision of Christ, so that now we may "regard no one from a human point of view." That means that if we are to live in the Spirit, we can no longer live a separate life, concerned only about our own well-being, because all that we do affects others and affects the planet on which we live. In Christ all is one.

That reality gives new meaning to the oft-heard imperative, "Love your neighbor as yourself," which is repeated in Scripture, from Leviticus to the gospels to the letters of Paul and James. Multiple examples are given as to what this teaching implies: clothing and feeding those in need, not coveting our neighbor's goods, being hon-est in our dealings, forgiving others' wrongs. The list might go on to include even the most ordinary everyday actions, such as smiling at a clerk in the grocery store, expressing concern for a sick friend, listen-ing to those who are worried, simply giving our attention to those who call. We participate in a very real way in the suffering and joy of all, for unity shines through duality.

The consciousness of our immersion in unitive reality causes us to love ourselves also, for Christ lives in us. True love of self is only pos-sible as we grow to know ourselves as one with Christ. Cherishing ourselves, how can we neglect our bodies, our need for rest, relax-ation, and enjoyment? How can we neglect our souls which cry out for times of quiet and meditation, which yearn for spiritual nourish-ment? Overwork, stress, and fatigue so often consume our energies that we forget who we really are and who our neighbor is. Then we move in a day-to-day routine that blinds us to the wonder of the life we live, and robs us of the energy to live life to the fullest.

Jesus' life on earth offers us a blueprint of what it means to be Christian. We are called both to live by the words he gave us and to act as he acted. Yet this goes far beyond imitating his actions; it means living his life, allowing him to live through us today. Although this may seem to surpass our capability, it is possible because we have received his Spirit, and with it the graces of "love, joy, peace, patience, kindness, generosity, faithfulness, gentleness, and self-control" (Gal

5:22). When we fall short of our desire to manifest these qualities, the remembrance that it is possible helps us to begin again and again. We live Christ's life as human beings with the emotions, physical limitations, and shortcomings that are common to all of us. It is in that context that we have been invited to share in the divine life; God knows us more deeply than we know ourselves.

Watching for indications of that unitive reality as we allow the words of the gospels to unfold in the warmth of our heart and as we spend time savoring the parables of the kingdom, pondering the letters, praying the psalms, can have a remarkable impact on us. Scriptural prayer can inflame us with the fire of the Holy Spirit, so that we become the fire.

Praying psalm 139, we can immerse ourselves in an assurance that God understands our deepest desires to live Christ's life.

> O Lord, you have searched me and known me.
> You know when I sit down and when I rise up;
> you discern my thoughts from far away....
> You search out my path and my lying down,
> and are acquainted with all my ways.
> Even before a word is on my tongue,
> O Lord, you know it completely.

If we allow the words of that psalm to move into our hearts, we can experience greater calm and a profound trust, in spite of our failings, because a loving God who knows our innermost being sees our desire as well as he observes our every action.

As we enkindle our desire to live fully in this new dimension by remaining close to the word of God in Scripture, grace can penetrate our defenses. Christ, the Word of God, can become ever more consciously an intimate part of our lives. Then it will become easier to see everything and everyone with the eyes of Christ, and we will begin to see Christ in all, including ourselves. That perspective opens us to an awareness of the world in which we live, a world shimmering with the glory of God! Whether we see the sparkle in a child's eye as she looks at a Christmas tree, sit at the bedside of a dying friend, or watch the full moon rise over the Mediterranean, we will remember that

If anyone is in Christ,
there is a new creation:
everything old has passed away;
see, everything has become new! (2 Cor 5:17)

6

The Unitive Light

Inner Transformation

In the beginning was the Word,
and the Word was with God,
and the Word was God.
All things came into being through him,
and without him not one thing came into being.
What has come into being in him was life,
and the life
was the light
of all people.
The light shines in the darkness,
and the darkness
did not overcome it.
John 1:1–5

Imagine that you are walking into a dark room. As you carefully feel your way to avoid tripping or bumping into things, you gradually discover a footstool, an armchair, and a low table. Then you finally find the lamp and gratefully turn it on. Suddenly the room is filled with light! Objects you only found one by one as you groped your way through the darkness are illuminated and brought into a single vision in which you see the whole room. As the light fills the room, it unifies all that once seemed separate. Its physical, sensible presence transforms obscurity into clarity. This is an experience which is such an integral part of our lives that we forget to marvel at the miracle.

The analogy of light has even become a part of our everyday language. Have you ever said to someone, "It just dawned on me that I had an appointment today"? Or found that as you were reading a poem, the meaning suddenly dawned on you. Then again, a friend might say to you, "I finally saw the light!" Realization, insight, and understanding are often expressed by the metaphor of dawn, light, or vision because the sudden, intense light of the intellect draws everything into focus and allows us to see the whole, to see more than one idea at a time. That is why when we understand a complex principle, we exclaim, "I see what you mean!" Words falter as we try to describe the mysterious illumination of our minds that so spontaneously makes it possible for us to grasp a concept which until then lay in the darkness, beyond our understanding.

Light is an elusive, intangible, and yet intrinsic presence in both the physical and the intellectual aspects of our lives, but its source—divine, uncreated light—is infinitely more incomprehensible. That is the light to which John refers in the prologue to his gospel where he writes, "The true light, which enlightens everyone, was coming into the world" (Jn 1:9). We are bathed in that light, even as we are filled with it. It emanates from within us. It is that light to which Jesus refers when he says, "I am the light of the world. Whoever follows me will never walk in darkness but will have the light of life" (Jn 8:12). That light is like the spring of living water that wells up within us and overflows into every aspect of our life.

Jesus is telling us the unimaginable truth that whoever follows him will share in his divine, uncreated light and will be united by that light with the very life of God. This awesome teaching can fill us with delight and plunge us into dread, a sacred dread that leaves us fearful yet enthralled as the awareness of who we are and who God is gradually unfolds within our hearts.

Those thoughts, that reality, cannot be grasped by the human mind alone, but they can be savored and held in the heart as they ripen in the warmth of divine union. Our immersion into divine life is only accessible to us through baptism which initiates us into full participation in that uncreated light. That is so easy to say, but so difficult to comprehend, so challenging to live!

Paul realized this paradox when he expressed his hope to the Colossians that they might have "all the riches of assured understanding and have the knowledge of God's mystery, that is, Christ himself, in whom are hidden all the treasures of wisdom and knowledge" (Col 2:2–3). We can know Christ only through grace, a gift which is always present, but which we must freely accept. Paul told us that as we live our lives in Christ, we "have come to fullness in him" (Col 2:10). Yet, he also knew that our awareness of the divine life we share would not develop immediately and automatically, but that we would have to make an effort to develop our perception of it. This limitation is a part of the human condition.

We do, however, live in the radiant light of divine mystery which continually unfolds in our lives. If we remove the veil from our eyes that we may see, we will live in a state of unending astonishment. We will come to know the eternal beauty of God that Gregory Palamas, a fourteenth-century theologian, describes as a superluminous splendor:

> The very formless form of the divine loveliness,
> which deifies man
> and makes him worthy of personal converse with God;
> the very Kingdom of God, eternal and endless,
> the very light beyond intellection and unapproachable,
> the heavenly and infinite light,
> out of time and eternal,
> the light that makes immortality shine forth,
> the light which deifies those who contemplate it.

In writing this passage he struggled to find the words to describe the eternal beauty of God. It was the light with which Peter, James, and John were surrounded when Jesus was transfigured before them, "and his face shone like the sun, and his clothes became dazzling white" (Mt 17:2). At that moment Jesus was not changed, but the eyes of the three apostles were opened to divine reality. Palamas writes, "They indeed saw the same grace of the Spirit which would later dwell in them; for there is only one grace of the Father, Son and Spirit." It is this same grace and eternal light which illuminates all baptized Christians. For that reason Jesus could say to his disciples, "You are the light of the world....Let your light shine before others, so that they may see your good works and give glory to your Father in heaven" (Mt 5:14, 16). The parallel statements, "I am the light of the world" and "You are the light of the world," reveal clearly to us that we live in Jesus.

Most of us were too young when we were baptized to realize the transformation that took place in us, and most of us still fail to grasp the immensity of that transformation even as we mature. I do, however, remember distinctly that on the day of my confirmation, when I was twelve years old, I truly expected to be different after receiving the sacrament. I thought that I would feel a mysterious, new strength. So, as I walked out of the church that afternoon, I stopped on the steps for a moment to experience the difference. The scene is still vivid in my mind. It was an old, mission style church that opened on to a beautiful park. I stood there, looking at the beauty before me, and slowly became aware that I felt exactly the same as I had felt when I went into the church! I must admit that I still feel the same, but I am gradually realizing ever more deeply the amazing change that did come over me when I was baptized and confirmed.

In order to begin to grasp the depth of the significance of the divine light that dwells in us, it helps to remember the creation account: "Then God said, 'Let there be light'; and there was light" (Gn 1:3). God said, he spoke the Word in which "all things came into being" (Jn 1:3). Later, these words came into fullness when Jesus, the Word of God exclaimed, "I have come as light into the world, so that everyone who believes in me should not remain in the darkness" (Jn 12:46). He is the uncreated light which now illumines all who believe in him. The gradual unfolding of this revelation, and of the astounding revelation of our oneness with Jesus and with his Father, sheds new light on all that we are and all that we know.

In the Scriptures, wisdom is described as "a reflection of eternal light" (Wis 7:26). In Isaiah we read, "Then your light shall break forth like the dawn" (Is 58:8). And to the prophet Esdras, Yahweh said, "I will light in your heart the lamp of understanding" (2 Es 14:25). The psalms are also replete with references to light:

The unfolding of your words gives light. (Ps 119:130)

The Lord is my light and my salvation. (Ps 27:1)

In your light we see light. (Ps 36:9)

Your word is a lamp to my feet
and a light to my path. (Ps 119:105)

Notice that when these words were written, the Word of God had not yet come to share in our humanity, and so make it possible for those who believe in him to share in his divinity. At the moment of Jesus' resurrection, a door was opened for us. If we choose to walk through that baptismal door, we are transfigured in the unitive light of God and participate in its mystery. That unitive light fills our being and shines through our flesh so that all we perceive can be seen in the rays of that light, and all that we touch is touched by God. I am reminded here of the words of the Sufi poet, Hafiz, found in his poem "When I Want to Kiss God."

When no one is looking and I want
To kiss
God
I just lift my own hand
To
My
Mouth.

On Mount Tabor, after Jesus' transfiguration, Moses and Elijah who had stood at his side disappeared, the light faded, the bright cloud lifted. Peter, James, and John looked up and saw "only Jesus" (Mk 9:8). That phrase has always fascinated me. I used to read it literally, feeling the apostles' disappointment that the vision had not lasted and that they had to return to their ordinary way of life. Perhaps I identified with what I perceived as their inability to see beyond the humanity of Jesus.

Yet with the eyes of faith, seeing only Jesus is enough, for in him we can see his divinity and see all those who, by sharing his life, live in him. The wonder of it is that if we can remember that we, too, abide in him, we can also learn to see with his eyes, so that everything will gradually fall into perspective, will be perceived in relation to the Divine. It is almost as if we were offered magical, mystical glasses that make it possible for us to see everything that happens brought into focus.

We know from experience, however, that it is not that easy. Internalizing our union with Jesus so that it becomes a vibrant force in our life is usually a slow, sometimes painful, process. It is possible through grace, however, because Jesus is the light which shines in the darkness of our ignorance, weakness, and suffering. He is the light which gives meaning to all that is, and we live in that light. We are the deaf who now can hear, the blind who now can see!

If we nurture our faith in these truths, they will become an inner force that invades our whole life. It not only brings us joy but induces us to reach out to touch God in others. Prayer and reflection on the revelations in Scripture enable us to penetrate more and more deeply this central mystery of our incorporation through baptism into the very life of God, never understanding it but knowing it.

Jesus came into the world as the "light of all people," that we "may have life, and have it abundantly" (Jn 1:4; 10:10). That light of divine life shines now in the darkness of our world and, in the words of Gregory of Palamas, it "deifies those who contemplate it."

7

The Golden Thread
Authenticity

Blessed are
the poor in spirit...
those who mourn...
the meek...
those who hunger and thirst for righteousness...
the merciful...
the pure in heart...
the peacemakers...
those who are persecuted for righteousness' sake.
Matthew 5:3–10

Last week I began to reflect on these beatitudes in preparation for writing this chapter. They seem to be a concise recipe for living the Word in one's daily life, and thus embodying and spreading the fire of the Holy Spirit. But how can this be realized? This listing of the qualities which assure one of possessing the kingdom of God can be so overwhelming that one is tempted to continue reading, unable to concentrate on the possibility of developing one quality or the other. My thoughts flowed in all directions, searching for a focus, a virtue which might lie at the core of each of them and make it easier for me to consider them.

Even as a summary of the gospel teaching, the beatitudes are an enormous topic. There must be a shared thread of gold that holds them all together but can be discovered only by returning again and again to the words of Scripture and by clearing away the clutter in our minds that hides the central teaching.

Then, over the weekend I was plunged into a paradoxical experience, and confronted with an opportunity to probe the meaning of the beatitudes in real life. I attended a national conference in San Francisco at a luxury hotel ironically named after the Poverello of Assisi, St. Francis. My window looked out on Union Square in the heart of the city. I watched a mélange of tourists and well-dressed business people hurrying past those less fortunate who spent the day on the park benches and, perhaps, their nights on the cold cement in doorways. Were these latter ones the poor to whom the kingdom of God had been promised? Or were the former the poor ones in another sense? Or is it only by looking into each one's heart that we could know which ones were truly the poor in spirit? In the midst of luxury I saw multifaceted poverty!

The theme of the meeting was healing, a topic that attracted both healers and those in search of healing, the merciful and those who mourned their loss of health. Yet all of us seemed to be isolated into hermetically sealed compartments, each one focusing on learning as much as possible from one speaker and then rushing to the next speaker. There was little thought of speaking to each other. This lack of connection is one of the epidemics of the modern age, and I found myself caught up in it. Which of the qualities listed in the beatitudes might heal that isolation?

Even as I walked through the hotel lobby or sat in the coffee shop for a light meal, I was aware of the dichotomy of values. We had gathered to listen to the wisdom of those who had much to share about various modalities of healing, but were we listening to the woundedness of so many persons around us? Of course, it was not the time to intrude upon others' lives, but were we even aware of the neediness in our midst? Were our hearts sensitive enough to listen and to heal by an authentic presence in a superficial environment?

My reflections on the beatitudes have been enriched by that weekend experience which brought my prayer into focus with reality. Scriptural reflection should never be separated from the world around us. It must touch the ordinary moments of our own lives and be colored even by the news of the day, the events of the entire world, for the word is a living Word that speaks even today.

As I returned to my writing, I began to glimpse at least one golden thread that runs through the eight descriptions of those who are blessed. It is authenticity, living according to one's inner truth, without pretense and regardless of the consequences. This authenticity or integrity is a prism that transforms the light of that truth into rays of many colors: poverty, simplicity, meekness, mercy, purity, an endless spectrum. Each color is a pathway to the blessings of eternal life. If we are authentically who God created us to be, we will be poor, merciful, and meek. That, however, leads to another question: what do each of these qualities imply? How am I to be poor? What does it mean to be meek and pure of heart? If we are to understand these virtues as Jesus meant them, it is important to return to the gospels.

Many of Jesus' teachings, which Matthew clustered together in the passages now referred to as the Sermon on the Mount, were drawn from the vast reservoir of the Hebrew Scripture and placed in the context of the new law. The beatitudes at the beginning of the discourse echo the themes of psalms, prophecies, and wisdom literature, which in many instances referred to the role of the Messiah. It is challenging, however, to translate Hebrew words of those writings because each carries a wealth of meaning which imbues them with a depth that cannot be expressed by a single Greek word, the language in which Matthew wrote. Hence, some of the original Hebrew words are expanded in the beatitudes to express more than one quality.

Actually, the evangelist Luke includes only four of the eight beatitudes recorded by Matthew (Lk 6:20–22). Scholars believe that only the first three of those may have been spoken by Jesus at one time, and the fourth spoken closer to Jesus' prediction of his passion. The other four recorded by Matthew may be glosses, or further developments of the original three, which were added by the evangelist for the sake of his audience.

If we follow that analysis, we are left with "blessed are the poor, those who hunger and thirst for righteousness, and those who weep now." Further reflection might even lead us to conclude that it would have been enough for Jesus to say, "Blessed are you who are poor, for yours is the kingdom of God" (Lk 6:20). This would have been feasible because the word for poor that is often used in the Hebrew Scriptures familiar to the Jews is *anawim*, a complex word to translate because it has so many nuances. Perhaps that allows Matthew to broaden the concept of poor to the poor in spirit, a phrase which extends the concept of material poverty to include an inner sense of poverty.

There is an example of this word in the book of the prophet Zephaniah where we read,

> Seek the Lord, all you humble of the land,
> who do his commands;
> seek righteousness, seek humility;
> perhaps you may be hidden
> on the day of the Lord's wrath. (Zep 2:3)

The Hebrew word anawim, translated here as humble, also means "poor, oppressed, afflicted, or meek." According to a footnote to this passage in the Jerusalem Bible, among the Israelites those described by this adjective were also considered to be those who submitted to the will of God and were thoughtful of others. As we read in the prophecy of Isaiah, it was to these very people the Messiah would be sent.

> The spirit of the Lord God is upon me,
> because the Lord has anointed me;
> he has sent me to bring good news to the oppressed,
> to bind up the brokenhearted,
> to proclaim liberty to the captives,
> and release to the prisoners. (Is 61:1)

The word translated here as oppressed is the same word translated in the passage from Zephaniah as humble. Interestingly, when the passage is included in Luke's gospel, the word given here as oppressed is translated as poor.

This passage played a significant role in Jesus' life for it described the Messiah and, of course, was the very passage read by Jesus in the synagogue one Sabbath in Nazareth. After reading it, he sat down and said simply, "Today this scripture has been fulfilled in your hearing" (Lk 4:21). That statement must have had the effect of a lightning bolt shooting through the synagogue. This man from Nazareth, their own neighbor, claimed to be the Messiah! To the listeners who, although they could see, were blind to the truth, this was blasphemy. Furthermore, it threatened their own status and would turn their world upside down if it were true. In their fury at such a claim, they drove Jesus out of town and tried to throw him off a cliff (Lk 4:29).

Jesus had come to the synagogue shortly after returning from his forty days in the desert, where, after overcoming the temptations of the devil, he had been "filled with the power of the Spirit" (Lk 4:14). He then had begun preaching and was well accepted by the people until he came to his own town and revealed his identity. He was more than the carpenter's son, he was the Messiah who had come to fulfill what had been promised to them, but they did not want to believe him.

Jesus' reading of the text from Isaiah was the turning point in his ministry, for now the people either accepted or rejected him; there was no middle ground. He was no longer a man who gave inspiring sermons that they could listen to and easily forget, because now he claimed to be the anointed one sent by God. If we place Jesus' words referred to as the Sermon on the Mount in that context, the beatitudes stand out as more than a list of virtues which will be rewarded. These were the words of one who spoke with authority and said very emphatically, "Blessed are you who are poor, for yours is the kingdom of God." It is also revealing to note that it was not by chance that Jesus opened his sermon with statements that referred to the very ones to whom he had been sent. Only the Messiah, only the Son of God could present us with the kingdom of God. His very presence brought that kingdom into the world.

In the gospel of Matthew the gift of the kingdom was explicitly promised only to the poor in spirit, perhaps because one who is truly poor is also empty enough to hunger and thirst after justice, is pure in heart and merciful. Those who are poor in spirit are not only externally poor and without possessions, but experience a profound sense that even their innermost qualities are gifts of the Spirit. They mourn not only for themselves but for others, and often are the peacemakers among us, the nonviolent.

The blessed ones referred to by Jesus have emptied themselves of artificiality and pretense. They have nothing more to lose, and so are able to come closer to an authenticity and integrity of spirit which allow them to experience true freedom and to be themselves. It may be that quality of authenticity which lies at the heart of each of the beatitudes, the golden thread which ties them all together.

Perhaps Jesus, and later the evangelists, enumerated more than one quality of those who would be blessed because in our human approach to sanctity it is so much easier to focus on specific virtues than on only one commandment such as "love the Lord your God." If this were not the case, Jesus might have simply said, "Blessed are those who love God"! Then too, as unique individuals each of us is usually called to develop certain facets of spirituality more than others. For example, there are those who are active in works of social justice, many who embrace the joys and sacrifices of raising a family, others who minister to the sick and needy, some who embody pain and suffering, while others choose the renunciations integral to a monastic or a contemplative life. One need only remember the lives of the saints to note the unique quality of each one's response to God's love. All of these ministries are expressions of the virtues listed in the beatitudes. Each of the beatitudes is an opening to the others, and a pathway to the kingdom of God, because each is a manifestation of poverty of spirit and of integrity.

Authenticity might even be considered one of the golden threads that weave through all of Scripture. Yahweh's resounding "I am," spoken to Moses from the center of the flaming bush, spirals through the universe as a burst of authenticity and integrity: "I am who am" (Ex 3:14). God is. Nothing more need be added to that revelation, so the words of revealed Scripture circle around that one reality, unveiling for us the infinite facets of the one divinity. Notice the many occasions in the gospel of John when Jesus appropriated to himself those same words, "I am" (e.g., Jn 6:35; 8:12; 8:58; 10:7; 10:11; 11:25; 14:6; 15:1).

Moving ever more profoundly into this truth, we too become more integrated so that our fragmented self falls into kaleidoscopic order. Gradually, we begin to perceive everything that exists as intricately woven into one tapestry. When we no longer conceive of ourselves as separate and alienated from the rest of creation, we are free to be more truly who we are. Then enormous love and compassion begin to take root in our heart, for love of God, self, neighbor, and creation slowly merge into one. We begin to know the oppressed, hungry, homeless, and suffering ones of this world as a part of ourselves, as an expression of divinity, and in them we know God.

As we immerse ourselves more consciously in the revelation we encounter in Scripture, the realization of who God is, who we are, comes into sharper focus. The truths that we have professed to believe for so many years take on flesh, come alive, become an integral force in our lives. We can no longer hold them at a safe distance, for we realize that we truly are intimately united with God.

That astonishing, awe-inspiring recognition introduces us to an interior dimension of ourselves where we are more receptive to the energies of divine grace. We intuitively know that which is beyond comprehension, so that we speak our name with Yahweh from the center of the burning bush. We are fire!

Participating in this reality, we become open channels of divine love, so that as we touch others' lives through our daily activities, thoughts, and prayer, we will spread the divine flame. Our lives then will take on new meaning. Nothing is insignificant; all that we do manifests God's love.

Epilogue

It
Is often
Nothing the Master says
That keeps the desired fire in me
Alive.

Wherever the Master goes
An invisible pile of wood tags along.

That he keeps throwing logs from
Onto my

Soul's hearth.
(*"An Invisible Pile of Wood," Hafiz*)

Yesterday I finished typing the last chapter just as twilight arrived, a quiet, sacred time on a cold, rainy day. It was an evening that called for a warm fire in the wood stove. It seemed appropriately symbolic that I should relax before a fire as I reflected on the thoughts I had just written. I put the kindling and logs carefully in place, lit the fire, and sat quietly, enjoying the colorful, dancing flames that seemed excited to be alive!

I, too, am a fire, thrilled to be aware of my oneness with the flame of divine love. Yet I so easily forget the reality in which I live, which I am, and move among the moments of the day as if everything were mundane, so ordinary. Then my flames become embers waiting to be enkindled once more, but they never die.

Soon I had to get up to tend the fire in the stove, rearrange the logs, and add another. Fires are that way. They continually call for attention. Is it any wonder that the fire within me also needs to be fed, lest it become only glowing embers? This reminded me of one of my favorite poems by Hafiz, the Sufi poet who so artfully weaves the ordinary with the divine. I can visualize God throwing logs from an invisible pile of wood onto my soul's hearth, never tiring of tending my fire. Those invisible logs are all of the unexpected thoughts, feelings, and emotions that call me back to an awareness of God; the beautiful scenes of nature, the acts of kindness, and even my own neediness that can startle me into a remembrance of the divine; the words of Sacred Scripture that encapsulate the divine fire and return me to a conscious participation in the life of God.

So as I sit before the vibrant, luminous flames in my wood stove on this rainy evening, I am filled with grateful awe that I am. My prayer for all of you who read these words is that you also may experience the wonder of who you are, who God is, and the realization that "between God and the soul there is no between." We are all united in the fire of the Spirit.

Come Holy Spirit,
fill the hearts of your faithful
and enkindle in them
the fire....

References

Arseniev, Nicholas. *Mysticism and the Eastern Church.* Crestwood, New York: St. Vladimir's Seminary Press, 1979.

Barnhart, Bruno. *Second Simplicity.* Mahwah, NJ: Paulist Press, 1999.

Cassian, John. *Conferences.* (Colum Luibheid, trans.). Mahwah, NJ: Paulist Press, 1985.

Eliot, T. S. *Collected Poems 1909-1962.* London: Faber and Faber Limited, 1963.

Guigo II. *The Ladder of Monks and Twelve Meditations.* (Edmund Colledge, OSA, and James Walsh, SJ, trans.). Kalamazoo, MI: Cistercian Publications, 1981.

Grimm, the Brothers. *The Complete Fairy Tales of the Brothers Grimm.* (Jack Zipes, trans.). New York: Bantam Books, 1987.

Hafiz. *The Gift.* (Daniel Ladinsky, trans.). New York: Penguin Putnam, Inc., 1999.

Howell, Alice O. *The Dove in the Stone.* Wheaton, IL: Theosophical Publishing House, 1988.

John of the Cross. "The Ascent of Mt. Carmel," in *The Collected Works of St. John of the Cross.* (Kieran Kavanaugh, OCD, and Otilio Rodriguez, OCD, trans.). Washington, D.C.: ICS Publications, 1979.

Jung, Carl G. *Mysterium Coniunctionis, Collected Works Vol 14,* 2nd edition. (R.F.C. Hull trans.). Princeton: Princeton University Press, 1970.

Louf, Andre. *Teach Us to Pray.* (Hubert Hoskins, trans.). London: Darton, Longman, and Todd, 1991.

Palamas, Gregory. *The Triads.* (John Meyendorff, ed., Nicholas Gendle, trans.). Mahwah, NJ: Paulist Press, 1983.

Pannikar, Raimon. *A Dwelling Place for Wisdom.* (Annemarie S. Kidder, trans.). Louisville, KY: Westminster/John Knox Press, 1993.

Of Related Interest...

With Hearts on Fire
Rev. Joseph Donders

With Hearts on Fire is an inspiring series of reflections on Jesus and his proclamation of the reign of God. It looks at Christ's vision of that reign and what we can do to bring his vision to reality in our lives and in our world. A wonderful companion for celebrating daily liturgy as well as for reflecting on the weekday readings.

0-89622-974-2, 352 pp, $19.95 (J–22)

God's Word Is Alive!
Entering the Sunday Readings
Alice L. Camille

Offers solid material for breaking open every reading of all three liturgical cycles, for Sundays and holy days alike. Contains commentaries on each of the three readings, reflection questions and points for action, a liturgical calendar up to the year 2010, plus an index of Scripture readings in sequential order. This is both inspired reading and a most useful resource.

0-89622-926-2, 416 pp, $19.95 (C-02)

Prayer-Moments for Every Day of the Year
Mary Kathleen Glavich, SND

A wonderful collection of one sentence prayers, organized into categories. Drawing from the Bible, the saints, and the liturgy, the author packs a treasure chest of short prayers for every need, every expression of human emotion and of divine love.

0-89622-748-0, 80 pp, $7.95 (B-82)

Prayers of the Hours
Morning, Midday & Evening
James Richard Lahman

A book of three prayers for each of the 31 days that have relevant Scripture verses. The prayers are Christian, but otherwise non-denominational.

0-89622-677-8, 136 pp, $9.95 (M-55)

Available at religious bookstores or from:

TWENTY-THIRD PUBLICATIONS
PO BOX 180 · 185 WILLOW STREET MYSTIC, CT 06355 · 1-800-321-0411
FAX: 1-800-572-0788 BAYARD E-MAIL: ttpubs@aol.com

Call for a free catalog